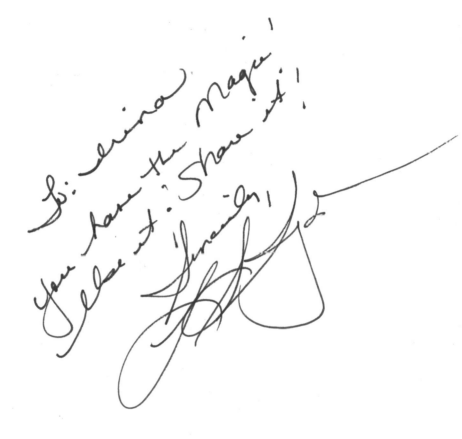

MENTORING

MENTORING

The Most Obvious Yet Overlooked Key to Achieving More in Life than You Dreamed Possible

A Success Guide for Mentors and Protégés

FLOYD WICKMAN
TERRI SJODIN

McGraw-Hill

New York   San Francisco   Washington, D.C.   Auckland   Bogotá
Caracas   Lisbon   London   Madrid   Mexico City   Milan
Montreal   New Delhi   San Juan   Singapore
Sydney   Tokyo   Toronto

Library of Congress Cataloging-in-Publication Data

Wickman, Floyd
   Mentoring: the most obvious yet overlooked key to achieving more
in life than you dreamed possible: a success guide for mentors
and protégés / Floyd Wickman, Terri L. Sjodin.
      p. cm.
   Includes index.
   ISBN 0-7863-1135-5
   1. Success—Psychological aspects. 2. Mentoring. I. Sjodin
Terri L. II. Title.
BF637.S8W47 1997
158'.2–dc20   96–41068

McGraw-Hill

A Division of The **McGraw·Hill** Companies

McGraw-Hill books are available at special quantity discounts to use as premiums and sales promotions, or for use in corporate training programs. For more information, please write to the Director of Special Sales, McGraw-Hill, Professional Publishing, Two Penn Plaza, New York, NY 10121-2298. Or contact your local bookstore.

 This book is printed on recycled, acid-free paper containing a
minimum of 50% recycled de-inked fiber.

8 9 0 DOC/DOC   0 2 1

*I would like to dedicate this book to my
ultimate mentor, my lifelong partner, Linda.
She lifts me up and keeps me humble, and
continues to teach me every day the meaning
of life, love, and how to enjoy the moment.*

Floyd Wickman

*To all my mentors who were generous enough
to share the pearls of wisdom which took them
a lifetime to learn, and to my family and friends
whom I continue to learn from and with.*

Terri Sjodin

CONTENTS

Chapter 7

Questions and Comments about Mentoring   139

Chapter 8

The Magic of Mentoring   157

INTRODUCTION

Is your life better than it was a decade ago? By better, we mean happier and more fulfilled, with a greater sense of personal achievement. It should be—much better. Take a minute to reflect on how hard you have worked to make it so. If you are better off, great! If, however, you feel you have *more* problems, *more* stress, *more* pain, and less time for your family and—more important—for yourself than you did just 10 years ago, well, we will say that we aren't terribly surprised. We have been hearing it from many others like you—hardworking people who are used to being successful but feel that things are slipping away from them. The fact is, many of us feel we just can't cope any more. It seems that the problems are still with us, but the personal accomplishment isn't.

Most of us see the future in terms of what has happened in the past. We realize we are struggling, so we look at how we overcame our last challenge, or the one 15 years ago. We overcame our problems then, so, with a track record of success, why can't we handle what's happening to us today?

We have been told that information is power. We see ourselves in an information explosion, so why do we feel increasingly helpless the more time we spend at our computers, sending e-mail, and acquiring an ever-increasing array of gadgetry? Is one reason because everyone else always has the critical information we are seeking before we do? Is it that improved communications means we now can fall farther behind *even faster* than we could before? It seems that if you stop to take a sip of water today you must spend a half-hour catching up with everything that occurred in the interval.

The new decade presents a number of challenges for the person who cares about personal success and achievement. By success we mean more than just financial independence, though we certainly include that near the top of our list. When we refer to success, we are talking about *personal fulfillment*. For some this will mean financial reward, but for others it will mean recognition by their peers, and for still others it will mean the attainment of a long-sought goal such as helping others. Most of us, as soon as we achieve success in one area, start getting restless. Then we begin setting a new goal. So success is an ever-moving target that requires constant striving and constant vigilance.

What is it that has changed in the new decade to make success, contentment, and balance appear so elusive? Even those who have achieved financial success feel personal fulfillment slip through their fingers. How can someone possibly be financially secure and not be happy? It does happen—it may have happened to you. "How can this be?" you ask yourself. "Is it a trick? I've practically killed myself trying to provide for my family, but I still have all these *problems*!"

Both situations are really two sides of the same coin. In the first, you feel unhappy *because* you are not financially successful. In the second you feel unhappy *in spite* of being financially successful. Let's face it: you haven't solved the problem. Could it be because you haven't clearly defined what the problem is? Or is it because you haven't changed your approach to life in light of your altered circumstances? We believe it very well may be both.

In our seminars, we like to tell a story we think captures the way many people feel about life today. Because it lets us view our circumstances from afar, it offers the beginning of a solution and perhaps a different perspective on change. We call it the cheese story . . .

> One day a laboratory scientist picks up a mouse from his cage and drops him into a maze. The mouse hunts through the interconnected pathways and, in about 15 minutes, finds the piece of cheese placed there by the scientist. The next day, the scientist takes the mouse, drops him into the maze again. This time the little mouse finds the cheese faster. This happens several more times until the mouse learns to go straight to the cheese without any false turns. He wastes no time exploring avenues that don't lead to a piece of cheese. He learns how to get where he wants to go. (Isn't this what we all want?)
>
> Eventually, however, the 90s arrive. The scientist decides he is going to change the rules. He puts the mouse down in the maze, and the mouse takes the same path he has always taken before, and runs over to where the cheese used to be. Surprise—it's not there! The mouse sits there in the hope the cheese will reappear, but it doesn't. Eventually, the scientist puts him back in his cage. The next day, the

mouse zips through the partitions, arrives at the other end, and the cheese once again is nowhere to be found. He keeps doing this over and over, still looking for the cheese. What happened? Well, it's very simple: *the cheese moved!*

Most of us, working hard all throughout the 80s, determined where the cheese was. We learned—for that period—which path to take to get to where we wanted to go. At the end of the decade, we were familiar with how to get from the start of the maze to the cheese without starving. Enter the 90s, and we begin to wonder if that is still possible. What has changed now since our cheese-seeking days of the 80s? Well, it's essentially the same thing: *the cheese moved.* The response most of us have to this dilemma is the same as the mouse's. We just continue to follow the same path through the maze that we always followed, hoping that maybe tomorrow—or the day after tomorrow—the cheese will again be where it's supposed to be! Well, in our humble opinion, it's just not going to happen. Ultimately, you have two choices. You can continue to take the exact same path and wait for the cheese—and possibly starve to death—or you can choose to change and find the cheese's new location. So what is the problem? It is difficult to learn any new route to a piece of cheese that may or may not still exist. Sometimes it seems as though it's almost easier just to go hungry than to begin searching for a new way through unfamiliar territory.

Where do you go to find the solution? There is hope, and it comes in the form of what we call "the final secret." Many of you already have taken classes in success and/or seminars in selling, and have attended workshops in stress management and organization. Have they helped? Sure they have. Have they helped enough? Probably not. You still feel as though you are sliding backward or at best not achieving the kind of success you want, you need, and you dream about.

Ironically, there are people who continue to prosper in spite of difficult times. Somehow they routinely know where to go to find the cheese. What makes them different from the rest of us? Is it intelligence, training, or perhaps natural talent? We believe that we know what it is, and it is none of these things. It's a concept that dates back thousands of years. We call it the "mentoring lifestyle"—the final secret. In its simplest form, mentoring is people helping people, but our research indicates it goes much deeper than that, is more spiritual, and considerably more focused. A local barn raising this is *not*. But the power of people helping people in a one-on-one, personal mentoring program can be the key to achieving more in life than you ever dreamed possible.

It is ironic when we describe mentoring as the final secret to success, or even as a secret at all. Mentoring has been around for thousands of years, so why is it such a secret? Where has it been that so few people today are taking advantage of it? The answer is that it has been lost under the clouds of social change, corporate restructuring, and political infighting. It is so simple that it has largely been ignored while we searched for complex solutions to crime, drugs, broken families, and care for the aged. The sad part about this is that we aren't employing this age-old secret for the same reasons that make us need it in the first place.

Like the master illusionists from the time of Camelot to the present day—the Merlins and David Copperfields—the successful people who hold the secrets don't readily reveal what they know or how they obtained their knowledge. People who are experts in their fields today—the top musicians, physicians, athletes, businesspeople, craftsmen, and, yes, even salespeople—simply don't tell the rest of us the hundreds of personal insights into how they arrived where they are today. If they did, we would be the beneficiaries of their wisdom and experience and would be better equipped to succeed at our respective endeavors. *We would know how to find the cheese.*

So how can you learn to perform like the great masters of our day? How can you learn their secrets? How can you acquire these closely guarded "pearls of wisdom" that distinguish the outstanding and successful people from the hoi polloi? We believe the answer lies in the time-honored tradition of mentoring. Only when you establish the relationship of mentor/protégé with someone more knowledgeable than yourself can you be "invited in" to learn the thousands of details that distinguish the outstanding from the average.

How do we know that mentoring is the final secret? We are living proof of the power of mentoring. We have done what many of you have done—the schooling, the postgraduate courses, the practice, the commitment—and yet the "magic" didn't all come together for us until we became involved with mentoring. Now each of us has been a protégé and a mentor to other people and known the fulfillment that comes from helping others progress to the next level. And both of us have known failure and heartache. The drive to overcome these crippling defeats, to achieve success, is what drove us to discover the final secret.

We have been friends for more than five years now in a working relationship characterized by the principles of mentoring. Although Floyd had been involved in mentoring for a number of years, having already recognized its importance in the achievement of success, it took Terri's proposal to co-author a book on the subject before we realized how significant mentoring has been throughout the ages. Floyd's decision to collaborate on a book dealing with the subject was based in part on the reaction he saw among his colleagues after telling them about the project.

> Everyone thought doing a book on mentoring was a great idea. At first, I was a little disinterested, though, because I didn't have a vision for another book. I recognized that I knew enough about mentoring to contribute a substantial amount of information, however, since I had been either a protégé or a mentor almost my whole working life. The second thing was that if Terri Sjodin says she wants to do something, she generally will do it. I've always been amused by her ability to swim with the sharks and was impressed by her previous books. So I reluctantly said, OK, I'm in. As I started researching mentoring to learn what other people knew about it, I began discovering things. At first I wondered if my own success and the connection I made between being a mentor and protégé was a fluke. Then I started checking with people like Zig Ziglar, Og Mandino, Brian Tracy, and Les Brown and found that throughout their whole working careers they have been involved in mentoring relationships, as mentors as well as protégés. Terri started bringing in some studies that got pretty exciting. Looking beyond my own field—the speaking business—you realize successful people from all walks of life—lawyers, doctors, models, athletes, actors, clergymen and more—all are and have been involved in mentoring relationships. All these people were protégés to mentors and mentors to protégés. Then it hit me. If *everyone* were a protégé to a more experienced mentor and a mentor to a less experienced protégé, how much better off we all would be!

Because of our personal experiences with mentoring and its impressive list of benefits, we both come prepared to provide a unique perspective on the subject that includes detailed descriptions of the two sides of the mentor-protégé relationship, Floyd from the mentor's perspective, and Terri from that of the protégé.

Floyd's rise to success is dramatic in view of the disadvantages he had starting out in life. Here is a brief overview of how his early adoption of the mentoring lifestyle changed his life from an underachiever, who nevertheless was still hardworking, to an example of success and inspiration for others.

> I was an abused kid who spent two years in the ninth grade before quitting school. For me the role was almost pre-established. You do drugs, and you run with gangs, and you go to jail. You spend 10 years in the Navy, and you attain a low rank. Then you have two businesses that fail and you declare bankruptcy. The irony is, *I've always been a very hard worker,* and I've always had the dream. But at age 26, I had nothing to show for it. Then I found my first mentor, and I learned to start giving. I mean I applied every principle I was taught, and these ideas did great things. My life changed when I heard Zig Ziglar say, 'You get everything in life you want if you help enough other people get what they want.' I also was reading Og Mandino's book, *The Greatest Salesman in the World,* reciting every script: 'I will greet each day with love in my heart . . .' etc. As a result, I am a giver of my time and knowledge. I've never kept any secrets. The funny thing is, I am also a lot happier than most of the other successful people in my field who haven't learned this simple lesson. These two men still have a profound impact on my life.

The mentoring lifestyle is one in which people share their time and their knowledge with those who are willing to perform the work required to become successful. Terri is one of those people willing to do the work, but she realized she needed more; she needed the knowledge of exactly how to turn that work into success. She needed a helping hand from someone more knowledgeable and experienced in her chosen field of public speaking. Here is her story of how she discovered the importance of the mentoring lifestyle.

> I've been in the sales training and development industry since the day I graduated from college. I've always been goal-oriented, but what I couldn't handle was how long it was going to take for me to get where I wanted to be through the traditional methods—the academic system and what's commonly known as paying your dues. I kept thinking to myself that there must be a faster way. So when I read *The Richest Man in Babylon* and learned what a mentor was, I decided that a mentor was what I needed. I knew that I wanted a mentor, but I didn't know how to go about finding one. When I spoke at the conference where Floyd and I were introduced, and he

offered to provide me with counseling and some guidance, I accepted. Because of Floyd and other mentors along the way, I have progressed toward where I wanted to go much faster than I would have otherwise. I'm still in pursuit of my dream, but because I have achieved so many of my initial goals fast, I find I have lots of younger people who ask, "How can I do what you have done?" I keep pitching the concept of getting a mentor. With the information we have now collected on mentoring, people are going to figure out in a few hours of reading what it took me seven years to discover. They will get it faster than I did so they can make success happen for themselves sooner. If they follow the tenets we are outlining, they also will be happier and more fulfilled as individuals.

This book has several goals. In it we will:

❖ Discuss different types of mentoring.

❖ Explore possible areas where mentoring has been found to be most useful.

❖ Provide social proof, not only statistically but through heartfelt responses from both adults and young people about how mentors have affected their lives.

❖ Discuss the benefits of being a mentor.

❖ List the qualifications for becoming a mentor and a protégé.

❖ How to select a good mentor or protégé.

We also will take a look at the 16 Laws of Mentoring. These are the pearls of wisdom gleaned from our many years of experience with mentoring and from the input of readers and researchers. The laws are the summation of the basic principles on how to successfully manage a mentoring relationship.

All this is offered in the hope that once you are exposed to the wonderful mentoring lifestyle, you will become excited enough to start thinking seriously about how mentoring can play a part in your life, either by serving as a mentor or becoming a protégé—or ideally, *both*. (We will be switching back and forth between the two points of view so you will come to understand both perspectives.) Earl Nightingale said that you become what you think about, and we want you to start thinking about how mentoring can become a part of your life. We will discuss some of the myths and problems associated with mentoring so you will be better prepared for managing your own mentoring program.

Along the theme of family values, we will take a look at how parents, grandparents, and family members serve as mentors and why traditionally they have been among the strongest mentoring influences in many people's lives. Despite the large number of single-parent households today, we believe that we will see a renewed commitment on the part of family members to help each other find personal happiness and success as we move into the latter part of the 90s and beyond.

Finally, we will provide a number of stories and letters recounting "magical" mentoring relationships. These are accounts of individuals who have had a lasting impact on the lives of others. We hope these dramatic and moving stories persuasively proclaim what we believe are the benefits of mentoring will inspire you.

This book answers the question, What is the secret to achieving success on your terms whether it be personal, professional, economic, or emotional. The answer is found in the following truth: *If every person in our society served as a mentor to a protégé as well as became a protégé to a mentor, we would be more successful and capable of solving our problems substantially faster than we do today.*

The final secret to success lies in adopting a mentoring lifestyle. This is more than just a mind-set, however. It means making a commitment and taking action. We will give you the tips, show you all the tricks, and provide you with the tools you need to begin a journey that, hopefully, will last the rest of your life. Along the way, you will find your failures less painful, your achievements more rewarding, and your whole life experience more positive than you could any other way. You only have one life to live. Why not make it shine through adopting a mentoring lifestyle.

ACKNOWLEDGMENTS

I have always believed that "when the student is ready, the teacher appears." Literally thousands of people have taught me something that "made a difference" and made this book possible, but there are a few I would like to mention here in particular.

First, and foremost, thank you to my loyal staff. They watch my back, they protect me and make me look good, and they always come through; but I especially want to thank them for becoming experts at handling what we affectionately call UFOs (Unexpected Floyd Objectives.)

Thank you to my coauthor, friend, and protégé, Terri Sjodin, who helped me believe I had something of value to offer.

Thank you to all the protégés I have worked with over the past 30 years. Some I have heard from, and some I have heard of. But for a few, I have heard both *from* and *of* them. These are the protégés I am especially proud of because they showed me they care by keeping in touch, and they had the courage to go out into the world and apply what they learned. Thank you all for making me a better mentor.

And finally, to all my mentors, thank you. I must thank Zig Ziglar, for the hundred times he took my call, and with the patience of a saint, guided me toward becoming a more professional speaker. And I must thank Mark Murray for many years of no-nonsense business advice and selfless friendship.

Floyd Wickman

I would like to thank Chris Smith of CC Communications, Long Beach, California, for his efforts editing and rewriting this material. It helped blend Floyd's and my two very different sides of the story—the mentor's message and the protégé's perspective. It was a challenge and a major undertaking. The easier way to have done it would be to write one book on how to be a protégé and another on how to be a mentor, but we believe they are two sides of the same coin. To write a book covering both perspectives really took a third person to help bring them—and us—together.

The second person I want to thank is my assistant, Mary Jo Standley. She has been instrumental in helping me to compile and organize material and was invaluable in maintaining links with the contributing authors. She always did a wonderful job managing this information when I was away on trips. I am deeply indebted to Mary Jo for always letting me vent. She has stood by me listening patiently and later reflecting as I have expressed myriad emotions.

Obviously, I want to thank all the mentors who have helped me to get to the place that I am now. Floyd, Don Martin, Jim Roe, Nido Qubein, and Jerry Anderson.

I would like to thank all of the members of the National Speakers Association, people who submitted their stories and shared ideas, philosophies, and concepts that helped us to compile this book and make it the multifaceted work that we wanted it to be.

My friends and family were—and continue to be—part of everything I do, and their support is vital. Great goals are fun to achieve, but they mean little if you don't have people with whom to share your success. They are the ones who make it worthwhile and really make life fun.

Terri Sjodin

1

CHAPTER

Mentoring—A Close Look

A mentor is someone who helps us learn the ways of the world, someone who has our best interests at heart.

MENTORING—PAST AND PRESENT

Mentor and Telemachus

The Introduction has set the stage for why you might need help in achieving your goals in the 90s and beyond and given you an idea of mentoring. We also have shared our personal experiences with the mentoring lifestyle. Let's briefly examine why we call mentoring the final secret.

When Odysseus, the king of Ithica in ancient Greece, went off to fight in the Trojan War, legend has it he left behind his trusted friend, Mentor, to look after his son. The young boy, named Telemachus, was without a father for more than 10 years while Odysseus first fought the Trojans, then wandered for a decade in a journey recounted by the poet Homer in his epic tale *The Odyssey*. The word mentor—meaning a wise and trusted teacher or counselor—has been with us ever since.

A mentor is someone who helps us learn the ways of the world, someone who has our best interests at heart. The difference between

1

a mentor and a teacher is that usually a teacher is paid to train us in a specific discipline, whereas a mentor is a friend who gives time and knowledge without asking for anything in return.

A mentor's student is commonly referred to as a protégé, generally a younger person interested in learning all that the mentor has to offer. The protégé is someone the mentor regards highly enough to consider worthy of his or her time. This type of relationship between mentor and protégé has been honored for thousands of years.

The Richest Man in Babylon

In his famous book, *The Richest Man in Babylon,* written in 1926, George S. Clason uses a mentor named Arkad to illustrate the principles of accumulating wealth. Babylon became the wealthiest city of ancient times because its citizens appreciated the value of money and espoused sound financial practices. The city had been poor when the king asked Arkad to serve as a mentor to the citizens by sharing with them his "cures for a lean purse." His informal teachings caught on at a time when the city was searching for answers. There were no universities then, and mentoring was a way of passing on valuable know-how.

Mentoring developed into a widely practiced means of furthering the education of promising young people as human knowledge exploded during the Renaissance. It was widely practiced in the artistic and scientific communities, where it retains a traditional presence. As reading became a skill shared by the masses, however, and publishing provided an outlet for every conceivable idea, mentoring gradually grew less significant. Who needs to be indebted to a single individual when you can read the opinions of many? Mentoring later was adopted by corporations as a way to train young managers until downsizing engulfed corporations in the early 90s.

Mentoring was thriving in the 1970s, but by the early 1990s it had taken a near mortal blow in corporate life. Senior executives had undergone changes in corporate life that they didn't understand and had difficulty explaining to their subordinates. Executives began to work so hard that no time was left for activities like mentoring. The now thinner ranks of management were deeply affected when anyone left, and there was little desire to help train someone only to see them quit. Large numbers of women entered the managerial ranks. Mentoring activities that used to take place after work around a cocktail or on weekends at the golf course were eliminated. There were too many issues to contend with when mentoring crossed gender lines.

Yet mentoring is experiencing a resurgence in general interest today. Its premature uncoupling by corporate America has left a big gap not yet filled by other means. Mentoring today merits special attention in our rapidly changing technological society.

FOUR REASONS (AMONG MANY!) MENTORING WORKS

1. Experience Is the Best Teacher

There is a reason why mentoring continues to survive over hundreds of generations. No one can argue that experience is the best teacher when it comes to learning. While reading about something or seeing it on television is interesting, having another human being explain it to you and answer your questions is a time honored and preferred means of learning values, skills, and information. And usually there are so many details involved in the average job today that only someone who has been there and done it really understands all that is involved.

A mentor is someone who has experienced what you are trying to learn. He or she knows the pitfalls. If you are clever enough, you probably could figure out on your own much of what a mentor can teach you. But how long would it take? You might get there eventually, but why go through that taxing process when someone already knows the answers to your questions? We are reminded of a *New Yorker* cartoon showing a businessman in a tattered suit, holding a patched briefcase, his hat crumpled and hair a mess. An onlooker whispers to his colleague as they pass, "There goes a self-made man."

2. The Amazing Benefits of Synergy

Synergy is the ability of two or more people to achieve an effect that each is incapable of alone. Mentoring works partly because two people, if well matched, can create more energy and accomplish larger goals than one person can alone. The power of synergy is well documented and comes into play in many ways in the mentoring process. You can use this synergy with your mentor or protégé to accomplish things you never would have attempted alone. It is a powerful force and one of the many reasons why mentoring is so effective today.

3. Perpetuating Positive Action

The ancients knew numerous secrets that have become lost during the course of time. The way the Egyptians prepared and preserved their dead is still a mystery. The secret to the magnificent sounds produced by a Stradivarius violin disappeared forever when Antonio Stradivari died. The great magician Houdini mastered many illusions that went with him to the grave. And many other secrets that would benefit humankind have been lost with the deaths of their discoverers.

The mentoring process allows the secrets, tips, and tricks of an accomplished master to be passed from one generation to the next without the information finding its way into the public domain. It provides assurances to the mentor that his or her hard-earned knowledge will be preserved yet not made available to everyone. That secret fishing hole you took your son to you may now want to introduce to your grandson, but you don't necessarily want to publish it in the local newspaper.

A protégé has the responsibility of picking up the baton previously carried by the mentor and carrying it to the next runner on the track. Through the mentor's decision to pass on the knowledge acquired in the course of a career, he ensures the positive effects of his actions will continue without him.

The Winning Futures Organization has promoted mentoring for many years and has a successful track record. This nonprofit agency matches high school students with adult mentors who serve as positive role models for the youngsters. The arrangement provides the youths with an extended family and helps shape them into more rounded individuals.

So the perpetuation of positive influences in mentoring relationships is not confined just to business but is present in other areas of society as well.

4. Part of the Natural Transition of Life

Mid-career people typically have been the ones most interested in becoming mentors. It is part of a person's vision of his or her life to be able to pass on what they have learned over the years. Mentoring someone can be pivotal in various stages of a person's career and gives individuals a chance for introspection and reassessment. It is sometimes seen as an acknowledgment that a person's life is half over. Some feel it is essential to mentor and develop another person in order to move on to the next stage of their own careers. The protégé becomes a reflection of their career, and therefore the selection of the right protégé is very important to the mentor.

AN ILLUSTRATION OF A MENTOR/PROTEGE RELATIONSHIP IN THE PRESENT

How does all this relate to you? What benefit can you incur from knowing how people who appear more talented and successful have managed to leverage their existing advantages? Our personal story is a classic example of how a mentor/protégé relationship can evolve and benefit both individuals over time. While we provided a brief overview in the introduction, we feel it is important to give you some specifics to the story. It started back in 1990 when Terri, an aspiring trainer and public speaker in her mid-20s, had a booth at an industry trade show where Floyd was speaking.

THE FIRST CONNECTION

As I watched Floyd, I thought, wow, this guy has timing. The audience is on the edge of their seats. He's got a ton of product (books and tapes) at the back of the room. That's what I want to do. I want to be respected like that. I thought, now that I've seen this example, I want to learn what this guy has to say and how he got where he is. Even before we met, I was asking people, who is that guy? When I introduced myself to him at the break, I was nervous but I was determined to learn everything I could in the short time I had. He was really busy and had a million people who were trying to talk to him. He said he

continues

continued

would stop by my booth later and take a look at my product and see what I had. I thought, sure, I'll bet! But he did stop by and asked me if he could have a copy of my workbook and brochure. I remember later that he kept teasing me because I was writing down everything he said. Whenever he gave me advice later, I would always call him back and say, "I did what you told me." That always seemed to impress him.

Floyd's recollection of his first meeting with Terri indicates he was impressed by her eagerness to learn and the professionalism she showed.

I still remember clearly after finishing a speech at a trade show the day this young, very professional looking lady walked up to me and said, "I want to know what you know." I had two immediate reactions. First, I never had anybody ask me for advice quite that bluntly. Second, I couldn't help but think, "Sure, if I had a nickel for every time someone walked up to me and said they wanted to learn how to be a speaker, only to never hear from them again, I would be a richer man."

I remember walking over to Terri's booth, picking up a copy of her book and her brochure and being immediately impressed with her professionalism. Unlike many ground-floor speakers, it seemed like she was doing the basics right, so we sat and talked. At that time, she didn't ask me to be her mentor, she just started asking my advice and impressed me with the fact that she was writing down everything I said.

Ironically, one of Floyd's lessons from an early mentor, J. Douglas Edwards, was: Write down every bit of advice your mentor gives you. Terri was doing that instinctively because she was determined to learn the secrets of being a professional speaker. To that end, she pursued the relationship with Floyd, and that follow-through impressed him.

What I also liked about Terri is I would quickly get either a follow-up phone call or a note explaining to me what she did with my advice. After several months of informal questions and answers, we decided to make the relationship more formal and agreed between us that I would be her mentor. She came out and asked me if I would do it, but mentoring takes a lot of time; there is risk involved. I wanted to see just how serious she was, so I put her to the test. I was doing a talk in Alberta, Canada, and I decided that would be a perfect place to test just how serious she was about taking my time and energy. My program assistant happened to be ill and couldn't make it, so I said, "Look, if you will fly for no pay to Alberta, Canada, and be my program assistant—make sure the room is right, sell my products, make sure the limousine picks us up

continues

concluded

on time, etc."—menial work from her point of view—"I'll consider being your mentor." I fully expected her to decline, but to my pleasant surprise, she said yes. She went on the trip, helped me out, and we talked, and she asked a lot of questions. That was the beginning of our formal mentor/protege relationship. I later invited her to give a presentation to my in-house staff in Troy, Michigan, and she did a good job.

She later impressed me so much that at my annual Master Sales Academy in Las Vegas, where I normally would hire renowned speakers, I had a slot that I thought Terri could fill. So I hired her for that event, and she was a big hit. She since has been invited back for two more appearances.

Floyd continued to support Terri as she struggled to make a name for herself in the competitive field of public speaking. Once, on her way to New Jersey after an exhausting road trip throughout the East Coast, Terri was so burned out that she was questioning whether or not all the stays in countless hotel rooms was a lifestyle she could stand. The intense travel schedule, the lonely road-warrior way of life, the discomforts for weeks at a time were taking their toll.

For Terri even to consider giving up her dream was an indication she had neared the end of her rope. She called Floyd's office in Michigan. Floyd was out of town, but Terri reached his operations director, Debbie Williams. Terri couldn't hold her feelings back any longer and poured out her frustrations to Debbie.

"I love the work, but I don't know if I can handle the grueling lifestyle," Terri confessed in the most mournful expression of personal doubt she had ever known. Within 10 minutes of that call, Floyd, who was halfway across the country, was on the phone to Terri. Debbie had called him en route via mobile phone as soon as she had hung up.

Recalls Floyd: "She was suffering. I knew what she was going through because I had been there myself many times." At that moment, Floyd shared with her one of his "pearls of wisdom," an insight that got Terri looking past the present. The lesson was this: "The nonstop road trips are all part of paying your dues," he said. "Once you make a name for yourself, you can pick and choose your schedule dates."

When Terri arrived at her hotel in New Jersey, there was a basket of fruit and bottle of champagne waiting for her in her room. Attached to it was a note from Floyd. That kindness and encouraging insight were enough to reinvigorate Terri's belief in herself and get her past a crisis that might have seriously impacted her career. She went on to establish herself as one of the youngest speakers on the corporate circuit today.

The mentoring relationship between Floyd and Terri has matured over the past five years. Floyd says that Terri isn't the only one who has benefited.

> Has it been worth it to me? The answer is a resounding yes! First, I found that by mentoring Terri on a wide range of areas such as speaking engagements, client relationships, and operating a speaking business, it forced me to become more effective. I can remember saying to Terri not long ago that I believe I probably earned an extra $100,000 just in the last couple of years just by following my own advice in the areas where she had questions.

Terri approached Floyd with the idea that they co-author a book. This publication —the culmination of their relationship—is a joint effort describing the magic of mentoring, a process they both have come to know and respect as being one of the most powerful forces they have ever encountered.

We hope that by sharing this story with you that you will be able to reflect on your own life and begin to overcome personal struggles and achieve more than you ever thought possible. The magic doesn't occur overnight. Every journey requires taking a first step, but even the smallest beginning can be the start of great accomplishment.

We have given you a brief look back at the origins of mentoring and its rise and fall in popularity in American corporations during the past few decades. We have also introduced you to how our own mentoring relationship was established and the perspectives we each had at the time that would lead us to assume the personal risks involved in establishing such a relationship. Let's now take a look at the lives of a few other people you may recognize and see how becoming involved in a mentoring relationship helped them achieve their dreams of success.

HIGHLIGHTS

❖ The word mentor derives from Mentor and Telemachus in Greek mythology.

- ❖ Mentoring was once widely practiced, particularly in the scientific and artistic fields.
- ❖ Mentoring survives because experience is the best teacher.
- ❖ Two people working together can accomplish more than each one individually (synergy).
- ❖ Mentoring is a way to pass information from one generation to the next.
- ❖ Serving as a mentor has the effect of enhancing a successful person's career.
- ❖ Terri and Floyd have shared how they developed a mutually beneficial mentoring relationship, with the hope that you will begin to see the process of how mentoring can work in your own life.

CHAPTER

How Mentoring
Creates Success

The reasonable thing is to learn from those who can teach.
Sophocles

We have brought you up to date on the history of mentoring, but
the question you want answered is, Can mentoring really make a
difference in my life? Can I do it? Is it really worth it? There are
going to be some of you who think that mentoring is a pleasant
enough idea in theory, and it sounds as though it *might* work, but
you aren't going to invest precious time in trying something new
unless you are *sure* it is going to work. Frankly, we wouldn't want
to waste our time—or yours either—on something that had not
been proven. This chapter is intended to give you enough information about successful mentoring experiences so that you will
feel confident about taking a chance regardless of what your goals
might be. We believe it is important to immediately begin developing mentor and protégé relationships. The world is changing
rapidly, and there is no better time to begin putting together your
system for staying one step ahead of those changes.

MENTORING BY DESIGN

Our first mentoring experiences came from reading the right
materials. This led us to visit the right places, which in turn helped

us to meet people who were suitable mentors. There was a significant element of chance involved. This book, however, is intended to help take that random element out of the mentor and protégé selection process.

Most people we interviewed or read about in the course of researching material for this book said that they found a mentor either because they were fortunate enough to work for someone willing to help them or through a friend or family member. Yet, there is instead a way to control the process of mentor (and protégé) selection, and in addition to eliminating the element of chance in finding a mentor, we will show you how to remove the need for having "to know someone."

This important chapter, which presents evidence that mentoring really works, provides you with a foundation for planning and goal setting. When you talk to the average person about mentoring, even one who has had a great mentor, he or she likely will say "I was lucky." We believe luck happens when preparedness meets opportunity. Our first mentor experiences probably did have an element of pure luck, but after that, these relationships were the result of setting goals and creating opportunities. We decided we were not going to wait and see if, by chance, we would get another mentor to help achieve our next goal. Once we had determined that mentoring works, and works well, we made a concerted effort to find someone who could help us get to our next goal sooner.

We want to take the luck out of finding a mentor or protégé. We want you to take what has been a chance encounter for a select few and turn it into a strategic part of your personal life plan. This approach works at least as well as the fortuitous encounters others have experienced, and often works better.

We also want to present you with a broader view than commonly held of the variety of areas in life where mentoring can prove effective. We want you to see not only how it can benefit you on a personal level but also how it can help society as a whole. By showing you examples of mentoring activities in nonprofit groups, large corporations, schools, and by people from all walks of life—federal officials, including supreme court justices and surgeon generals, all the way to top fashion models—we hope to establish beyond a shadow of a doubt that mentoring works on a personal level as well as a global scale to help human beings evolve into an ever more productive and creative world community.

Mentoring in Everyday Life

The nonprofit Big Brothers/Big Sisters of America organizations are deeply involved in mentoring. They match children from single-parent homes with adult mentors who serve as positive role models. Such figures are missing from the homes of many children today who hail from single-parent households. Most Big Brothers and Big Sisters organizations meet with their protégés on average three times a month, far more frequently than most other youth mentoring programs. An independent social policy research group, Public/Private Ventures, stated in an April 1993 report that the Big Brothers/Big Sisters organizations create relationships between mentors and protégés that last many years. What is the effect of this pairing up? According to the executive directory of the Big Brothers/Big Sisters of Santa Clara County, California, some 98 percent of the youths affiliated with the organization remain in school until graduation and don't have run-ins with the law. The organization attributes its success to a dynamic recruitment program that matches young people to appropriate adult role models, then offers continuous support from case counselors during the relationship.

Mentoring in Business

Managers Magazine, in its January 1993 cover story, featured an article about mentoring within the insurance industry. The story revealed the profound effects mentoring can have in a business environment. The article describes a study conducted by the Life Insurance Marketing and Research Association (LIMRA) that correlates in-house mentoring with productivity and retention of new agents during their first year.

Using a study group of 2,400 newly hired life insurance agents with no prior experience, LIMRA correlated their success with the presence of mentors. The study found that the survival rate among new agents with in-house mentors was 74 percent after the first year. However, among those without a mentor, the survival rate was a *full 10 percentage points lower—64 percent*. That means 240 agents failed during the first year when they might have become successful had they had a mentor to help train them.

The study went on to show that agents who had in-house mentors not only stayed with their new employers longer but, as we might expect, were also more productive. Those with a mentor averaged 35 life insurance sales. Those without an in-house mentor averaged only 30 sales—a difference of more than 15 percent. The authors of the study conclude that the improved success rate of agents with mentors was partly due to the fact they received better training than did the agents without mentors.

The report goes on to say that mentoring had an effect on the motivation of the new agents through development of self-confidence. "Agents with mentors have more confidence that they will succeed, and so they are probably more motivated to succeed," the magazine says. "Mentors apparently can be one *key component* for instilling the confidence and motivation that is so necessary for achieving success in new agents."

The study concedes it does take time to establish mentoring programs with experienced agents, but it endorses such an investment since the benefits justify the time spent. Failure to provide training in the form of a mentor or other support to new hires can lead to their leaving for another company or workgroup, the article said.

New hires are so hungry for training when they first start that if they don't get help from their immediate work groups they are likely to seek out whatever information they can get. This often is inaccurate, inappropriate, and can eventually lead to the defection of the employee to another job. The study presents a strong case why corporations should have in-house mentoring programs, particularly for new employees. The implication is that such programs would be useful in other corporate settings.

In the insurance industry, Richard McCloskey witnessed such profound results from mentoring that he built a company to promote the concept. Mentoring Systems, Inc., of Irvine, California, was established to help firms implement mentoring. Though the effort to incorporate a mentoring system should not be underestimated, successes can be impressive, as the following story given to us with the permission of Robert Brown (based on his article, "Million-Dollar Mentors Revisited," *Managers Magazine*, July 1991) so aptly demonstrates.

MENTORING PRODUCES MILLION-DOLLAR AGENCY

Michael White, CLU, ChFC, accomplished what many insurance agents only dream about. Within four years of starting an insurance agency from scratch, he built his Richmond, Virginia, brokerage into one that employed 22 agents and took in more than $1.1 million in new annualized premiums.

He also transformed his agency, that had earlier catered largely to the home market, into one selling mainly to business owners. Despite this elevation in clientele, White was able to hire a largely inexperienced force of sales agents. As his agency passed the $1 million mark, his four-year agent retention was holding steady at better than 70 percent.

White credits his success to a mentoring program pioneered by fellow Minnesota Mutual Life general agent Richard R. McCloskey, CLU, ChFC, CFP. The mentoring systems underlying McCloskey's $8 million agency provided White with the management structure, direction, and accountability he needed to achieve rapid growth while maintaining a lean staff. Today, White's strong orientation towards systems contrasts sharply with his reactive style early on. Practices White had followed to kick-start his agency and survive initially began to falter once he set his sights on long-term growth and profitability.

Like most managers, White thought he had good systems in place. In fact what he had was a patchwork with little consistency or direction. He realized that without the right systems, five years later he would be working just as hard but be no further ahead toward financial independence.

When Minnesota Mutual created a program to transfer McCloskey's highly successful mentoring techniques to other agencies, White was the first to sign up. The most obvious feature of the new methodology was pairing inexperienced new hires with successful veterans. Yet that was just one technique White adopted in an effort to reorganize his recruiting, training, and supervision. His goal was to accelerate the growth of recruits while raising the earning potential of more experienced agents.

White agreed to be accountable to McCloskey for results. He was expected to closely follow McCloskey's systems and meet with him at least quarterly to review progress. White wasn't promised a

continues

continued

panacea or any shortcuts to success. Instead he was assured of steady and substantial growth in exchange for a serious commitment and hard work. This mentoring program is not a system for a manager who doesn't like having his or her feet put to the fire. For the manager who is willing to adhere to specific instructions on exactly what, when, and how to do things, results are worth the effort.

By first setting various goals and deadlines, White created a sense of urgency within his business. The mentor program starts by placing pressure on the agency head to be organized and accountable. For White, that accountability started with recruiting, where he was to see the biggest impact. White had set annual recruiting goals, but hiring was intermittent and depended largely upon when a suitable candidate was identified. Under McCloskey's direction, White's recruiting program became highly organized. He started hiring only in conjunction with a set of semi-annual training classes. Start dates were established well in advance. When he pegged the target date for his first class of four agents, he didn't have any candidates lined up and only three months to identify and hire them. Fortunately, he found a pool of potential hires from his local college campus recruiting office.

If his current class was full, White would ask candidates to wait several months for the next one. Adhering to such hiring practices forced White to make difficult choices. His commitment to structure required him to risk losing good candidates he couldn't immediately accommodate. But the appeal of the mentor program also reaped dividends. Two agents he recruited in June were willing to wait for the next class the following February in order to join the agency.

White eventually hired a full-time trainer/supervisor, but initially those responsibilities placed heavy demands on him. One of the hardest aspects of recruiting for new classes was White's tendency to assume he couldn't handle any more inexperienced employees. Young agents constantly competed for his time, and agent-mentors were in short supply. Nevertheless, changes began to occur at his agency as a result of the new systems, changes that promised increased sales.

White not only began to get better organized as a result of the mentor program, but he also saw a vast improvement in the quality of his new hires. Several aspects of the program, including highly structured training, target marketing, and the opportunity for agents to "jump start" their careers by working closely with more experienced mentor-agents resulted in better candidates.

continues

continued

Most appealing to potential hires was the opportunity to work with a mentor in markets that held the potential for high commissions. Instead of having to work their way up into the high-end part of the business, new hires began cold-calling businesspeople from the start. Recruits set up appointments and accompanied their mentors to observe the sales process. This formal relationship could last up to a year and longer informally.

White jumped into the business market with both feet as part of his commitment to the new mentoring program. He knew it would take years to make the switch if he stayed in the comfort zone of the home market. But he understood how important it was to the long-term success of both younger agents as well as mentors to make respectable commissions. Business insurance offered that potential.

Within a short time, 88 percent of his agency premiums were being generated in the business market. White credited the goal-setting and accountability part of the mentor program as fundamental to his agency's growth. By starting agents in a target market, like business owners, White supplied and controlled the leads. Unlike a natural market, White could make sure agents never ran out of prospects to call.

In the family market, and before adopting the new approach, agents averaged only 25 calls and four first-time appointments per week. That compared to 150 calls and nine first appointments when working in the business market.

Structure was key to the program, and was first introduced to new agents during training. It later became part of the landscape. Computers, for instance, were available only between 11:30 A.M. and 1 P.M. and again after 5 P.M. By adopting this schedule, agents no longer diverted productive time away from prospecting in order to run financial illustrations.

Further, first-year agents were permitted only two activities— phoning or making appointments—between 8:30 A.M. to 11:30 A.M. and 1 P.M. to 5 P.M. This structure helped to focus activity and enabled White to keep a promise made during recruiting: "We're businesspeople and we work regular business hours."

The mentor program paid off for White's new agents. Two inexperienced candidates exceeded $100,000 of paid annualized premium within just a few years of starting and several more were poised for similar achievements.

continues

concluded

The program benefitted mentors, too. Sales plateaus became a thing of the past. White's first mentor, who reached a production record of $65,000 in annualized premium in the year prior to joining the program, within a couple of years climbed to $235,000, 70 percent generated by work with new agents.

Achieving million-dollar status for his agency in four years was made possible by White's unswerving commitment to proven systems. McCloskey made it clear to White from the beginning that his mentor program would not be easy but would virtually guarantee him a means to build a multimillion-dollar agency. With McCloskey as a model, White saw that the benefits of adopting and sticking with a system would pay off handsomely.

Corporate America realizes its next generation of workers is going to come from students attending high school today. Can similar results to those attained with new hires be achieved between industry leaders and the community at large? The answer is yes.

MENTORING POWER IN SCHOOLS

Corporations that finally understand the need for and positive impact of mentoring are now making an effort to become involved with students in "first-step" mentoring programs. For example, a recent article in *The Wall Street Journal* featured the following headline: "Mentoring in Schools Becomes Part of the Workday for Many Employees." The article discusses how businesses today increasingly let workers volunteer in schools to help improve students' skills. The hope is that placing a role model in the schools where students can listen to their experiences and ask questions will help teach school-age youths the value of getting an education.

Why are these companies so generous with their employees' time? In addition to wanting to cultivate a future workforce, these companies also want to find a way that they can contribute to the fabric of their local communities, knowing that giving back to the communities, in which they live is good business.

United Airlines, for example, will mentor an entire fifth-grade class at one inner-city school in Chicago. The company plans to stick with the children until they graduate from high-school. It clearly wants as many students as possible to go on to college and already is making plans on how to finance it.

At Snelling & Snelling Inc., Senior Vice President Brian Dailey serves as a mentor to high school dropouts, sometimes persuading them to return to school. When he discovered one boy had quit because classmates made fun of his clothes, Dailey put his money where his mouth was, buying him new ones.

Some firms, however, reportedly don't do much to publicize their mentoring programs, and there is a good reason for this. The fact is, they see the practice as a subtle but effective recruiting process. They look for students who are highly motivated to become involved in the programs on their own. Quite simply, they want promising students from their mentoring programs to apply for jobs with them as soon as they graduate.

MENTORING—IT MAKES A DIFFERENCE AT ALL AGES

Following is a letter we received from a young man who wrote us in response to our request to students to describe their early experiences with mentors. You can feel the sense of gratitude this person has for the individual who took the time to help him learn a little more about life. You also can feel the urgent thirst for knowledge and guidance as he begins to develop skills that will serve him in a very complex and competitive world.

SEEING THE BEST IN SOMEONE

My mentor will be a friend for life because she wasn't just a friend, but was much more to me. She always believed in me and she always used to see me messing up when I should have been doing good. She used to see me in gangs, with drugs, and hanging with the wrong people, but she said she always knew that she saw something good in me.

I didn't know what it was because I would go to school and work and, as she says, never really settle in or care for one thing or another. So she decided one day before my senior year to help pick me up.

continues

---

concluded

She encouraged me to go to school and try to graduate. She knew I needed a good partner to give me the inspiration to raise myself up. The sooner I noticed I was going to get something good out of it, the sooner I was going to feel good about myself.

First she started explaining to me what kinds of friends I had, what they were doing to me. She also said that the drugs were messing me up. I realized that these people were not my friends, and that I was messing up my brain. So she decided to take me out with her friends to distract me from all the bad stuff. She took me to the library to do my homework, which helped me pass my classes. She also kept my mind working on things that were good for me.

It has been a success because I'm not doing drugs anymore, and I'm not hanging out with the wrong people who are not good for me. Also, it has been a success since I passed most of my classes and I'm looking forward to graduation night.

I think sometimes you don't really know that what you are doing is wrong until somebody who knows you explains it to you, until they explain why every single thing that you are doing is wrong. Until then, you don't notice it. Also, they show you that you have a chance to leave behind everything that's bad for you and start all over again finishing what you have done so far that is good. They show you that you really could be happy. They show you that you could also make the person happy who helped you go through it and helped make you strong.

Tony Camarillo
Fullerton High School
Fullerton, California

GREAT MENTORS TO GREAT PEOPLE

Mentoring has been a theme throughout history, and it has been the mortar for many myths. Merlin the magician, whom we mentioned earlier, was himself the mentor of King Arthur, Aristotle was mentor to Alexander, and Carl Jung's great mentor was Freud. Joshua B. Adams, in an August 1994 article in *Town and Country Monthly*, summed it up with a line from Sophocles: "The reasonable thing is to learn from those who can teach." Regardless of which famous person you ask, you will invariably find they were mentored by someone. Here, based on Adams' *Town and Country* article, are accounts of several successful and well-known people who revealed the profound bearings their mentors had on their development.

Influencing a Brilliant Judge

The first woman to sit on the Supreme Court, Sandra Day O'Connor, chose law as a career as a result of the influence on her of a mentor she met at Stanford University. "I surely would have chosen a different path but for Professor (Harry) Rathbun," she said. " He held seminars at his home to discuss personal ethics and goals and how each of us can make a difference in this complex world of ours," said Justice O'Connor. "I decided to attend law school because he demonstrated so clearly that the law can be an instrument for social good."

Instilling a Famous Doctor's Urge to Excel

The former Surgeon General of the United States, Dr. C. Everett Koop, attained fame for the relentless antismoking campaign that he waged when he held national office. His unmistakable appreciation for mentors and the concept of mentoring can be felt in his recollections of the men who changed his life: "It was not until my second year at Dartmouth that I began to appreciate what a mentor was and how unique my relationship was with three remarkable men," he states. "Two were biologists, William Ballard and Norma K. Arnold, and the third, Ray Nash, was a typographer, broadly comfortable in the arts.

"They made things come to life, taught me how to express myself, made me want to excel," says Koop. "Ray Nash, for example, never let me have an opinion without explaining it—even why I simply liked one painting over another. And Norm Arnold helped me decide whether it was better to be the surgeon I had always wanted to be or the teacher who would enable young men and women to be the kind of surgeon I wanted to be."

A Distinguished Fashion Career

A highly successful American fashion designer and philanthropist, Bill Blass, was mentored by an editor at *Vogue* magazine named

Baron Nicholas de Gunzburg, or "Nicky" for short. Blass was working in the back room for another designer when Nicky noticed his distinctive designs as they were displayed. They met and spent years as friends. "Nicky wasn't one to give advice," says Blass. "But he taught you things about life. He taught you that invaluable lesson that it was important to take one's work seriously—but never be serious about yourself."

Nurturing Youth in the Competitive World of Modeling

Cheryl Tiegs, who parlayed a modeling career into a line of clothing, signature eyeglass frames, and a book on beauty was featured a couple of years ago in *USA Today* for her role as a mentor to young models. She received the Miss Clairol Mentor Award in 1993 for her encouragement and support of women. Her official protégé at the time was Lori Herbert, then 15, who has signed with the Ford Modeling Agency at the age of 13. Tiegs had committed to help Herbert guide her career. "There are many questions you have along the way," said Tiegs. "It helps to have somebody who has been through it." Tiegs credits three mentors for helping her achieve success: Julie Britt of *Glamour* magazine, Barbara Stone, her own agent, and Nina Blanchard, also an agent.

THE IMPORTANCE OF EARLY MENTORING

We wanted to talk with some of the nation's foremost experts in the field of success and motivational training to see what thoughts they might have about the importance of mentoring. We figured that since these people not only are personally successful but have made the study of success their life's work, they should know better than anyone where mentoring fits into the big picture of becoming successful. So we called them on the phone and asked if they had ever had mentors and what effects mentors might have had on their lives. The response was overwhelming. Not only had they all had mentors, but they strongly believed in the importance of returning the favor by serving as a mentor once they had achieved something worth sharing.

Typically, we only hear about a person's success after they have "arrived." What is interesting is that when you ask them how they achieved so much recognition, they almost always credit another person or persons who helped them realize their dreams. They are usually very grateful to these individuals and oftentimes humbled by the extreme generosity their mentors displayed.

From Rags to Riches

Les Brown is one of today's most highly acclaimed motivational speakers. He knows what it is like to work up from poverty to a position of national recognition. In a personal interview, Les shared his thoughts on mentoring and what it meant to him to have a mentor who believed in him.

My twin brother and I were born on the bare floor of an empty building in Liberty City, Florida, a poor section of Miami. There's no question that I'm a product of what could happen— not what should happen. Because of the vision someone else instilled in me, I am who I am today. If everyone had a mentor, I know it would change the world.

I think that we owe a debt. All of us are where we are today because somebody, at some point in time, saw something in us we may not have seen in ourselves . . . . None of us got to where we wanted to go in life all by ourselves.

Being a mentor is a way of repaying the debt to humankind and a way to share with others the benefits of our experience. It's a way to help them avoid making the same mistakes we did. Being a mentor is a way to let someone stand on your shoulders in order for them to go farther than they would have gone by themselves. My success is due in part to [nationally recognized speaker] Ed Foreman with Executive Development of Dallas. He took a liking to me and said he would help me. He become involved and sponsored me . . . He took me around and allowed me to see what he was doing. Then he gave me an opportunity with his clients—without ever seeing my stuff. He must have felt I had the ability to do it. We shared the stage together.

I also will never forget another major mentor influence—Mike Williams, the man who helped me to shape my message and who

continues

concluded

has been a mentor to me for many years. He helped me develop the various ideas I use in my presentation. I never could speak if Mike came into the room, and my staff knew enough not to allow me to do so. Even though we've been friends for over 20 years, he only first heard me speak in person two years ago. I simply could not speak in front of Mike. I held his opinion in such high regard that people would tell him afterwards about my presentation and he would give me feedback. He just unnerves me.

I did one presentation that I was particularly proud of; I felt really strong about it. I gave him a video of it and let him watch it. "Mike," I said, "tell me what you think." He didn't say anything at the time.

One day we were going for a walk. I said to him, "I guess I should just throw that videotape away?" I'm sure he'd thought carefully about his critique. He knew I was sensitive about what he felt.

"No," Mike said. "You should keep it. Use it for reviews so you will know what *not* to do next time." He was sensitive in delivering the bad news.

If everyone had both a mentor and a protege, I think the results would be dramatic . . . Hopelessness is the genesis for desperate behavior. Coaching, positive examples and relationships—having someone say, "There is a way you can make it"—can begin to reduce society's ills.

Look at a man as he is, and he becomes worse. Look at him as what he could be, and he becomes what he should be. That is what a mentor does: a mentor looks at you as what you could become.

Becoming a Top Sales Trainer

Tom Hopkins is one of the nation's leading sales trainers. He is a highly sought after speaker who appears before thousands of people every year. He also has been a mentor to a number of today's most popular and successful speakers, including Floyd Wickman. Hopkins feels blessed by the help he got from J. Douglas Edwards. Although Hopkins never had the advantage of a formal education, he acquired a lifetime of wisdom from someone willing to share his secrets of success.

I really believe that a mentor can have a tremendous effect on your life. I'm very fortunate; as a young person with a low self-image and no formal education, I had the good fortune to go into sales and meet a man named J. Douglas Edwards, the father of American selling. Back in the 50s and 60s, almost every major company relied on his fundamentals for how to go about closing a sale.

When I was 19, I attended a three-day program he gave, and he took a liking to me. I didn't have a suit to wear, but I plunged into real estate. When I began, I wore a black and silver band uniform. Edwards took a liking to me because I had the guts to go into what was considered a middle-aged man's business. Edwards became my mentor. I studied under him. After eight years, when I was ready to leave real estate in 1972, I drove to Phoenix intending to take advantage of an opportunity to invest in real estate. Ironically, I moved next door to him. I never had a clue that he lived anywhere nearby. I truly believe the connection between us was meant to be. I spent many a weekend at his side listening and learning. Before he passed away, he and his wife let me purchase the rights to all his material.

Mentoring is coaching: taking people who have the ability, and who are willing to discipline themselves and pay the price, and teaching them the ins and outs of the business. I have been a mentor to numerous speakers over the years. I think the first was Danielle Kennedy. After a successful career in real estate, she decided to be a sales trainer, the only woman at that time in the real estate field. She did a one-day program opposite me. We encouraged her toward speaking, and she developed wonderfully.

I have always believed that successful people are successful because they aren't afraid to share and help others grow. I've always been very open. I feel that if you have been given talent in an area, and society affords you an abundance of income and stature, part of giving back is to help search for those people who can help others.

Mike Ferry was just a young, new licensee when he worked for a real estate company that would bring me in to speak periodically, Mike took my three-day boot camp three times, and I feel that I mentored him. Brian Tracy, when he first moved here from Canada, spent time working with me.

continues

concluded

Many of my mentor relationships really aren't structured. It's almost as though you become friends. They have a challenge and call me, and I try my best to use my 30 years experience to delve into whatever I can do to help or advise them.

As a mentor, you must demand accountability and responsibility. I'll have people who really want me to work with them, and I say, fine, here's what I want you to do. I want you to get an inexpensive camcorder and have someone in the audience tape your presentation. Then send me the tape so I can take a look at your delivery, body language, and presence. And of course I wait, but if I don't get it in 60 days, they aren't willing to take the step, and they have written their own ticket.

If people were willing to spend time and effort to develop their fellow man, and the whole process was designed so people could live happier, more fulfilling lives, I think the effect would be overwhelming. Our world needs people who are willing to teach, to share. I think it would be very healthy for everyone who achieves stature and a position of leadership or financial prowess to reach back and say, "Let me help a few who need it."

MENTORS IN DISGUISE

Often the magic of mentoring shows up in ways we don't recognize at the time. A mentor can sometimes serve as a guardian angel, stepping in when most needed. Only later do we realize the significance of the gift this mentor has bestowed upon us. The following story from Dr. Gary Silverman best illustrates how important these mentors can be, oftentimes without our realizing it until years later.

A TALE OF TWO TEACHERS

I had wanted to be a doctor for as long as I could remember. There were so many reasons. As an adult, the reality of a career often tarnishes the dreams we hold as a youth. I can honestly say, however, that medicine has been everything I dreamed it would be—and more.

This achievement was important not only because it was the life-long accomplishment of my dream, but also because it took a lot of

continues

continued

blood, sweat, and tears to get there. For me, the harder the challenge the sweeter the victory. Becoming a doctor was the ultimate challenge. My college pre-med advisers told me I didn't stand much of a chance of getting in—about one in 3,000. After years of hard work, the decision as to whether or not I would be admitted to medical school rested in the hands of two teachers. It was incredible.

I started dreaming of a medical education when I was in high school. I spent a summer in a program for gifted students. I attended in the operating room and made rounds with the doctors. All of them were wonderful teachers and role models. This propelled me toward my dream.

As an undergraduate, I struggled at Duke University, competing with some of the top pre-med students in the nation. I nearly gave up. No matter how hard I tried, I couldn't get better than Bs in many of my science classes. These were good grades at Duke, but not good enough to be admitted to medical school. In my junior year, I undertook an independent study with a psychology professor, whom I will refer to as Dr. E. The project included performing surgery on rats. The results were less than optimal. I worked hard, but the experiments just didn't turn out. Since I had worked with him for a year, I asked Dr. E., if he would feel comfortable writing me a letter of recommendation for medical school. I gave him an out by saying, "If you feel you can't, please don't." He assured me he would write me an outstanding letter.

During my senior year, while taking a course in religion, I met one of the saintliest professors I ever encountered. He became more than my professor; he became my mentor as well. Everyone on campus adored Dr. Jones. He lived his religion. I learned much from his counseling and even more through his examples. In the fall, after my applications were already in the hands of the admissions committees, I spent an hour with Dr. Jones in his office just chatting. I was worried that after years of striving, I would not get into medical school. Basically I was looking for counseling. With a twinkle in his eye, he asked me if there was anything he could do to help. I said, not really, all the recommendations were in, the papers were filed. All that was left was to sit back and wait. He assured me, "As long as you have done the best you can do, no one can ask for any more." I felt relaxed just talking with him, as if an angel had just blessed me. Little did I know—one had.

continues

concluded

In the spring, I was accepted into medical school. I returned to thank my professors and advisers who had helped me reach this long-sought goal. In retrospect, the look I received from Dr. E. was one of unusual surprise. At the time, I just brushed it off to his being taken aback by my gratitude.

Not until years later, when I was having a friendly luncheon conversation with the dean of my medical school, did I learn the story of why I was accepted. He first asked me how I had got along with Professor E. I answered that we got along fine, as far as I knew. He told me Dr. E. had written an awful letter that nearly prevented my being accepted. It turns out he tried to torpedo my acceptance without my knowing about it.

The dean, who had himself graduated from Duke, reviewed the letter and decided to call one of his most trusted friends at Duke—Dr. Jones. Even though I had not asked for it, Dr. Jones gave me a glowing recommendation. My mentor's support came without asking. Not only did my A+ in his senior course on the Old Testament (that would not even be acknowledged in my admissions materials) impress him, but he told his longtime friend he felt my desire to be a physician was for all the right reasons. In short, he unequivocally recommended me, thus clinching my admission.

It amazes me how you can set your eyes on a dream, work for years to reach it, then have some person or event which you are unaware of change your destiny. It taught me that in spite of the many times we try to control our fate by doing all the right things to get a job or degree, it doesn't work. Just as often as not there is a mysterious force working behind the scenes, sometimes for good and sometimes with malevolent intent. I believe that what is meant to be is meant to be, and fate takes us to places without explanation. Somehow, we all reach the correct destination in the end.

I will never forget that particular day I chatted with Dr. Jones and was given a gift. It is a gift for which I will forever be grateful. As for Dr. E., I hope whoever was going to write a letter for *his* son to get into medical school was far kinder and more honest than his father was with me.

MODERN-DAY MENTORING

Countless stories and examples of the power of mentoring pervade every walk of life. We hope this chapter gives you the incentive to move forward in your own quest. We have recounted but a few of the countless experiences that exist in the minds and hearts of Americans and people throughout the globe. Mentoring is a quiet force for good that has been operating for thousands of years, serving the function of passing knowledge and values down through the ages from one generation to the next. Is there any difference, however, between what has gone on over the years and the present day? Is there any reason to modify our behavior regarding mentoring when it has performed its assigned tasks adequately for so many years?

For the answer to that, all we have to do is pick up the daily newspaper. Crime, drugs, and poverty jump off the front page. There are millions of young people between the ages of 10 and 15 in America today. As one researcher put it, these youths are "fatherless, Godless, and jobless," and they are just entering that age group that is responsible for the vast majority of all reported crimes. What do you suppose is going to happen when these unskilled teenagers can't find jobs? Given the current situation in the United States, is the government really likely to step in with any sort of meaningful job training programs? Is industry going to shoulder the responsibility not only of providing these youths the necessary education they somehow failed to acquire in school but the basic values of society, which they should have learned at home 10 years earlier?

If ever there were a time to figure out a way to help the next generation, this is it. The broken families, negative media influences, and overwhelming materialism that characterize our society today need to be countermanded with a grass-roots movement that is simple enough for anyone to learn and put into effect on their own but effective enough to produce results so plain they can't be denied. That movement is mentoring, and you can put it into effect today in your own home, school, neighborhood, or business. The mentoring lifestyle in which everyone is a protégé to a mentor and a mentor to a protégé is one that has benefitted the educated elite for thousands of years. It is now time to take this powerful secret of success and apply it in the public domain.

A personal mentoring program can benefit anyone at any age in any level of society. No one is either too knowledgeable to be a protégé or too ignorant to be a mentor. And no one can argue that the problems we face today from a complex and overcrowded world are going to be solved by an elite group of leaders with deep pockets. We are increasingly apt to have to figure out the solutions to our problems by working them out together. The time has come for us to relearn how to give help and to get help on a very personal level. The individual mentoring program we will outline in this book accomplishes that with a minimum amount of training, but there are rules that must be followed in order for a mentoring program to work, and we will tell you what they are in the chapters ahead.

We have tried to show you in the last few pages how mentoring has led to heightened accomplishment for many people, from high-school students to a supreme court justice. It is a proven method of achieving success. Then why isn't everyone today involved in the mentoring lifestyle? For one thing, many of us haven't been exposed to mentoring. Studies show that people who have been protégés when younger tend to serve as mentors when they are older. We can extrapolate the converse—that people who have never had a mentor are less likely to devote their time to helping others.

In the next chapter, we will introduce you to a number of different types of mentoring and list several common areas of everyday life where a mentor could help you to achieve your personal goals.

HIGHLIGHTS

❖ A study of 2,400 life insurance agents showed mentoring greatly improved productivity and success rates among new hires.

❖ Many companies encourage mentoring as both a means of contributing to their communities and as an effective recruiting process.

❖ Young people today—and adults as well—express a longing for someone to take the time to help them achieve their goals.

❖ Many famous people attribute their success to early mentor experiences.

❖ Success experts believe we should repay our debt to the former generation by mentoring those coming up through the ranks.

❖ Many times the magic of mentoring shows up in ways we don't recognize at the time.

❖ The need for mentoring is greater today than ever before, and young people in particular require positive role models and guidance.

CHAPTER

The Many Types of Mentoring

All the greatest minds who ever lived await you in the library.
Dottie Walters

Now that we have given you examples of other people who have been helped by mentors, who have reached levels of success they never dreamed possible through the guidance and assistance of someone who took an interest in them, let's take a closer look at the *process* of mentoring—what it is and how it works. Let's also examine a few activities where having a mentor could be appropriate and lead you to setting and attaining new goals in many different areas of your life.

There are seven basic types of mentoring:

❖ Primary
❖ Secondary
❖ Structured versus informal
❖ Active versus passive
❖ Long-term versus short-term
❖ Group mentoring
❖ Momentary mentors

PRIMARY MENTOR

The first type of mentor is the one we think of as most important—our primary mentor. This is the person we focus on most, the person we ask first when it comes to any issue we can't handle. Our primary mentor is likely to change as we progress through the various stages of life, but he or she will be that person we talk to about a broad variety of questions. Miagi, the marshal arts expert in the movie *Karate Kid*, agreed to mentor young Daniel, who was having a little trouble earning the respect of his peers. The heartwarming film describes the mentoring relationship that existed between these two very different people as well as the costs and benefits to both. The following illustration from commercial real estate consultant and author Jerry D. Anderson, CCIM, shows how later in life his primary mentor truly changed the course of his life experience.

PRIMARY MENTOR

Five years into my professional real estate career I was wildly successful, doing all the big deals in town plus helping professional athletes accumulate wealth through investment. I learned a few things about work and life from some people back then, but I never looked to anyone specifically as a mentor. I was young, "self-made," and invincible . . . I didn't need a mentor. Or so I thought.

My whole life changed one tragic day in August of 1979 when the private jet of my new business partner crashed with both of us and all our business agreements inside. My partner was killed. I miraculously survived but suffered second- and third-degree burns over most of my body.

Lying barely conscious in my hospital bed, I was aware not only of the loss of my friend and partner, but also of my career. I had put all my eggs in one basket and was depending on this deal as my source of income for the next few years. My family depended on my selling abilities but one look in the mirror told me that was no longer realistic. My face was burnt and disfigured and my head was the size of a basketball. I didn't want to go outside much less work with other people. I was alone, depressed, and hopeless. I felt like dying in the crash would have been a more merciful fate than living the way I was.

continues

---

continued

After three or four months passed, my health began to improve but my spirits didn't. The drive and motivation that I once possessed was replaced by self-pity and loathing. I didn't care about my therapy because I had no hope for my future. And then one day everything changed.

Out of the blue I got a call from a man named Lou Thomas. Lou owned the largest and oldest real estate company in our town. He had been an all-American football player in college and he had put that drive and competitive spirit to work in his business career and personal life. He was well known in town as a civic leader and one of the town's wealthiest individuals. I had met him once or twice in the past, but our introductions had been brief as he was a busy man, playing the game well over my head. He had heard about my accident and decided to give me a call.

When I picked up the phone that afternoon, I didn't know how to react to what I heard: "Are you ready to stop feeling sorry for yourself and put your talents back to work?" No one, not even my loving wife, had challenged me as directly as this man I barely knew. With that phone call, Lou forced me to see that if I was ever going to get back what I had lost, I was going to have to get up and make it happen.

I worked with Lou over the next few months and eventually he asked me to join him in building a commercial real estate firm. Happy to be back at work and on my feet again, I jumped at the offer. Lou and I worked together over the next five years, and the firm we created eventually came to dominate the activity in the country.

I learned many things about business in those years. Lou taught me how to recruit salespeople, broker real estate, buy real estate for my own account, and plan for the future. In short, he taught me how to build and run a successful company. He taught me so well, in fact, that eventually I moved to a bigger city and started by own company.

I didn't realize it back then, but during those years I learned more than just business from Lou. I also learned a few things about how to live my life. Through the example he set, Lou taught me what it means to be a man. He taught me to never quit, to live every day with honor and integrity, and to believe in myself and my abilities. In fact, he said the words by which I try to live my life: "Life is precious so don't tiptoe through it with a lukewarm attitude. Find something you can do with enthusiastic passion, and do it!"

continues

concluded

As my business blossomed in the larger market, Lou and I kept in touch as much as possible. We didn't speak every day, but he was always by the phone to offer advice and words of encouragement. Whether I had a specific question about business or needed a tip on how to handle my teenage son, Lou was always there for me. Then disaster struck again.

One dark day in 1988 I learned that Lou's all-American college football body was housing multiple sclerosis. He had never told me because he didn't want me to worry, but by this time it had become so advanced that he could no longer hide it. In fact, he wasn't able to handle the day-to-day affairs of his business anymore and he was starting to lose his company and his family fortune.

I was terribly angry with Lou for not having told me sooner. By then, my business was going so well that it had taken on a life of its own. I was able to drop everything, return to the place I grew up, and help Lou get a handle on things. As the years passed, Lou's health continued to decline to the point he could no longer be involved at all. On the bright side, this happened at a time when his two sons were about to graduate from college and were mature enough to start learning the business. I was thrilled to have the opportunity to return the favor Lou gave me by taking his sons on as my proteges until they were competent enough to take over on their own. They still run the company today and I am happy to say it is doing better than ever.

During the time we were together, I never really thought of Lou as a mentor, just as a partner and a truly good man. When I reflect on it now, I realize that he did everything a mentor does: He recognized my potential, he set goals for me, he shared his wisdom and experience, and he always wanted the best for me. I miss him now but he will always live in my memory.

SECONDARY MENTORS

Whereas a primary mentor offers general help, secondary mentors are those we go to for specific areas of interest. They guide us through many different issues that might come up in life. The primary mentor might address all possible areas suitable for mentoring. Our primary mentor could address our career or profession, our education, family, spiritual and physical health, fitness, financial goals, social graces, ethical questions, emotional well-being, or even philanthropic questions. They scratch (then polish) the surface of all these areas.

A secondary mentor is a person who specializes in any one of these areas. We like to recommend that people have one primary mentor and a number of secondary mentors. Each of these secondary mentors specializes in different areas where you may want help. Our primary mentor is somebody we might meet with frequently, whereas meetings with our secondary mentors likely would be more intermittent.

STRUCTURED VERSUS INFORMAL

We divide mentoring programs into two basic categories: structured and informal. We recommend that you create a structured, *personal* mentoring system. Make a commitment to build your mentoring support system. Some mentors may assume a role that is very structured. They will give you a fixed list of things to do and then will follow up based on that list. Many of the mentors with whom you will work, however, are not going to be that formal. They are going to be considerably more casual. Your own self-discipline will direct the relationship because your mentor's attitude toward you will be informal. Maybe you will just pick up a pearl of wisdom here and there. Perhaps you don't have designated meetings or appointments, and you may not even have specific goals. Maybe you just chat and bounce ideas off one another.

Structure may also be ordained, as in a corporate mentoring program. A corporation might decree that a group of 10 people become mentors and that it's their job to ensure that a group of less experienced protégés achieve a certain degree of skill. This would be a structured versus informal program. Another implementation would be when a senior person within a company might randomly select somebody with whom they enjoy working. They feel there is good chemistry. It's not actively structured by the company, but it's still a company-sponsored program. You might also find a structured mentoring program in an organization like the Boys and Girls Clubs of America, or in the Service Corps of Retired Executives (SCORE).

SCORE offers a fairly formal and structured mentoring program for helping business people. Structured mentoring doesn't necessarily mean it is an outgrowth of a company. You might align yourself with an organization that has more of a structured mentoring involvement rather than a personal, one-on-one relationship.

Unstructured mentoring would be characterized by a more personal, more relaxed environment. It doesn't suggest a relationship that is any less productive. It merely outlines a different type of setting under which mentoring occurs. In structured mentoring there is a specific set of rules or standards—guidelines that comprise a protocol.

What we are suggesting for people who want to enhance their performance is to create a structured mentoring process in their lives. By nature, some mentoring relationships will simply tend to become more structured. Others, just because of human chemistry, will be more informal. Floyd has been both a primary and secondary mentor to a number of people over the last 20 years. His first attempts at meeting people's requests for guidance were made on a trial-and-error basis. The results of those early experiences were spotty. He realized there had to be some structure and discipline in the process—no matter how friendly and casual the tone of the relationship—in order for his efforts to be effective and have sufficient impact.

Terri and Don, her secondary mentor for writing projects, have a process they go through naturally. She and Don meet for lunch or for breakfast. The last time she met him was at 7:45 a.m. on a Friday— the first meeting in four months. They set an agenda for all the things she wanted to work on. They might talk briefly on the phone from time to time but really don't delve deeply into any of the issues.

She wrote down the five projects she developed and had begun working on since the last time they met. She also listed what had happened to each and where she thought she needed advice. At the same meeting, she brought several contracts she was negotiating that she wanted him to look over. She was interested in his opinion of whether there were any bugs she should look out for. Says Terri:

> We get a lot done in a short period of time because I know the process and the way it works. We get through all the courtesies— "Hi, how are you, great . . . tell me about your life"—in about 10 minutes, then we get down to business. We hash out a lot of intense stuff for about an hour. Once he has given me all of his advice, we

have about a half-hour of natural discussion before parting. It's tight scheduling because his time is very precious. Yet, he still makes time for me. It's just amazing. With all of his involvement in big business deals—mergers and acquisitions—he still takes the time to meet me for breakfast.

Sometimes I still ask myself why he does it. I think the answer is that he gets a kick out of it. He says, "Terri, you never cease to amaze me. I don't mind meeting with you because I like watching you grow. It's inspirational. I left you four months ago, and you said you were going to do these things, and now you have done them. Wow. Here are some things you need to look out for."

He likes to do it. It has become structured even though it is very informal. It is the way that I have found makes the best use of both his and my time. I respect his time. It's an informal relationship, but I structure the meetings.

You may not be in a structured environment or have access to a structured mentoring program, and your relationships may be informal, but that doesn't mean you can't instill some kind of structure in your informal relationship.

ACTIVE VERSUS PASSIVE MENTORS

Active mentors get involved in your life. They look out for things that will interest you; they call you every so often and ask how you are doing. They might ask, "Is it time for us to have a meeting?" They are involved. They are participative. They take action on your behalf. There are others who just keep an eye on you. They don't really initiate anything, but you know they are looking out for you. These are your passive mentors.

A passive mentor might be a momentary mentor. Maybe he or she leaves you with just a quick pearl of wisdom, and they are in and out of your life as quickly as you can blink. But they leave an indelible impression on you. Floyd has several people to whom he is a committed, active mentor. He knows they are looking for advice, counseling, and help from him. However, this doesn't preclude his providing guidance and support to others when asked. He has assumed responsibility for being available for people if they ask for help.

Floyd has been friends for years with motivational speaker Dottie Walters, who likes to tell people about her passive mentor—

Benjamin Franklin. She chose him because the writings and message that Franklin left for all of us serve as a guide for how Dottie wants to lead her life. In her office, she has a big picture of Ben Franklin and calls him her mentor. She constantly turns to his advice and defers to the wisdom of his writings. Even though she obviously doesn't have an interactive relationship with him, it's still effective for her. In passive mentoring, the mentor is not actively participating in the relationship, but still can have a profound influence on the protégé's success.

The following story submitted to us by Dottie describes what we mean by a passive mentor.

GREAT MINDS ABOUND IN THE LIBRARY

No car. No college education. No money. Living in a rural, chicken-ranching town with very few sidewalks, no babysitter, a small dry-cleaning business that was not making it, and a big mortgage payment. I wrote these on the negative side of the big piece of paper I laid out on our kitchen table.

Then I began the positive side. Two beautiful babies, a husband who had survived four major Marine Corps South Pacific battles and was home at last, love of writing, a wonderful journalism teacher in high school who had encouraged me to write articles, poems, features, and a shopper's column for the Alhambra High Moor. Plus, a solid determination that we would not lose our little home. But best of all the positives—a public library card!

I read every business book I could find at the library. With the help of the great voices in these books, I started a tiny advertising business, on foot, pushing my babies in a rickety baby stroller. I tied bed pillows onto it with clothesline rope.

When I arrived at the newspaper office with a sample of the shopping column I had written clutched in my hand, there was a big "No Help Wanted" sign in the window. I asked myself, "If they don't want employees, what *do* they want?"

"Advertisers!" The message came back loud and clear. I pushed my two babies inside and asked if I might buy advertising space for my shopper's column at wholesale. I would resell the space at retail, writing my little shopping paragraphs in an interesting and feature style. The difference between wholesale and retail would be my

continues

continued

profit. If I filled the column all four weeks in the month, I would earn the house payment.

The publisher said yes to my idea and even allowed me to pay for the first week's space at the end of the second week. This gave me time to sell the space, collect the money, and pay him for his share. He told me later he thought I would quit within the first week.

It wasn't easy. On the walk to town everyday, the gravel road ate up my shoes. I cut cardboard to stick inside the soles. I carried extra pieces in my purse to get me home. The wheel kept coming off the baby stroller. I just kicked it back on.

Not having any business experience, I read the library's business books with passionate interest. It was Frank Bettger in his book, *How I Raised Myself from Failure to Success through Selling*, who introduced me to his great friend, Ben Franklin. What a wonderful blessing it has been to have Benjamin Franklin as my mentor and business friend.

Franklin told me: "Dottie, when you hit a pothole, don't quit. Think of going another way. And remember, always talk of benefits to the buyer, not yourself." Sent to England by the American Colonies to have the hated British stamp tax repealed after the famous tea dumping in Boston harbor, Franklin called on Lord North. Kept standing outside North's door, Franklin's business card was returned by the butler: "We are never at home to the Colonies, nor Mr. Franklin," he was told curtly.

Franklin didn't stop there but immediately took action. He began calling on friends of the Colonies, carefully explaining the benefits to England of reversing the tax. He asked them to sign a petition he had put together titled, "The Stamp Tax on the American Colonies Shall be Reversed." Many did so.

Next he went to those members of Parliament who were occasionally friendly to the Colonies. Many signed. Last, he spoke to those who were not considered friends and showed them the long list of names on his petition. When they saw the list and heard Franklin recite the benefits to England, many of them signed too. Franklin now had enough signatures to get the issue before Parliament.

The day that Parliament repealed the Stamp Tax, Franklin was there. He said he was "properly solemn and businesslike." Since he wore the same suit for the repeal that he had worn when he was

continues

concluded

turned away by Lord North, he looked down and thought he noticed an odd phenomenon—his suit was smiling!

When I called on the Pomona, California, Chamber of Commerce to open a new territory for my advertising business, they told me I must apply to their "Secret Investigation Committee." I prepared recommendations and filled out forms. A week later I received a letter from the owner of the city's big department store, who was head of the "Secret Investigation Committee." It said they had turned me down.

I phoned and asked the chairman if I could meet with him. I thought I must have failed to comply with their rules. I had no criminal record, was a United States citizen, and had a sound business. I sat at his desk in a gold oak chair and said, "Please tell me the reasons so I can comply."

"We give no reasons," he said flatly.

I left in shocked silence. Once outside in my car, I heard Ben Franklin: "Think of another way, Dottie. Think . . ." I drove to the Pomona City Hall, asked to see the city manager, and told him my story. He was angry: "Pomona encourages free enterprise. I want you to tell that story to the city council." It seems the city gave the chamber of commerce a lot of money to promote new business and were on the verge of considering an increase.

I spoke to the council and explained the benefits to the city from my work, told them about my business, and gave them my references. They promised to help me in every way they could. The council approved my city license on the spot. My advertising business in Pomona flourished.

A few months later the Secret Investigation Committee Chair retired as head of the department store. I called for an appointment with his son, who had taken over the store. I sat in that same chair, wearing the same suit I had worn when his father turned me away. I spoke only of benefits to the store. The young man signed a large advertising contract and prepared a check for me. When outside, I looked down and saw the strangest thing: My suit was smiling!

All the greatest minds who ever lived await you at the library. Don't despair because you don't have money or education. If you can read, help is at hand. Believe me. If you come to visit my office you will see a large picture of Benjamin Franklin on the wall. It is a photograph of the famous Houdin bust. When I am troubled or in need of an idea. I look up at Franklin—I call him Ben. He grins at me, gives me wonderful business advice—and then he winks . . .

LONG-TERM VERSUS SHORT-TERM MENTORS

Long-term mentors may be mentors for life. Even if they are not, you certainly rely on them for more than just quick answers you might need under immediate circumstances. You are hoping they will help you develop, grow, and mature. A long-term mentor will watch as you progress towards your goals.

It is possible to have a long-term mentor who is not your primary mentor. For instance, you could have a secondary mentor whose specialty is in finance and who counsels you in financial matters. Perhaps he or she does it for a very long time, but is not your overall primary mentor in terms of general life principles. They are very specific in terms of their participation in your life. Your primary mentor is probably more likely to be long-term, whereas a secondary mentor is probably more apt to be short-term, but some people have secondary mentors from whom they constantly seek counsel.

Whether you are the mentor or protégé, when you get into a relationship initially, don't expect it to be long-term. That may come naturally, but don't bank on it. The future of a mentoring relationship is always uncertain. There is invariably an end to it at some point. Whether it will continue for a day, a month, or several years is impossible to predict at the start. The important thing to remember is that even a short-term relationship can have great value both to the mentor and the protégé. Knowing that they have helped someone, furthered another person's career, or perhaps averted a crisis in someone's life gives mentors a great deal of satisfaction. It is the way to give back some of the help they have received from others over the years.

We believe a person should enter into all mentoring relationships, whether as a mentor or protégé, assuming that they probably will be short-term, then see how the relationship naturally grows and develops. That way, you won't put a burden or unrealistic expectations on another individual. The beauty of working with mentors and/or protégés is that the relationships are flexible and just naturally bend with life. Mentors will be there when you need them and absent when you don't.

Long-term mentoring relationships are going to be more relaxed than short-term ones. We believe whether a relationship is long or short-term has a lot to do with an individual's chemistry.

You might need them in your life longer, and they might need you in their life longer. It's the constant rekindling of the relationship that makes it long-term. You might find that short-term situations served their purpose, but then the chemistry and the need for both of you wanes; you connect and quickly disconnect. You get what you both need, and then you move on to the next level.

For the protégé, the level of intimacy with the mentor may grow, but closeness has a lot to do with dependability. If you enjoy and respect the relationship and are getting the kind of coaching you seek, you will become more intimate.

The mentor is looking for feedback. If he or she sees progress in the protégé and hears the kinds of messages he or she is interested in, the relationship just naturally grows. The protégé can't just approach someone from the starting gate and say, "You are going to be my long-term mentor." It's not like a marriage where you commit for life. And even when you do have a long-term mentor, at some point it may be important to move on and find someone else. That person may have been your mentor through a long process, but then you drift apart. Or perhaps you don't like the direction in which one of you is going. There really is no way to put a time limit on a long-term relationship, but we can arbitrarily say they last in excess of three years.

One of Floyd's first protégés spent several years learning and growing in a mutually beneficial mentoring relationship with him. Eventually he went on to achieve success in the field of training and development and later enhanced Floyd's business by becoming a member of the team of Floyd Wickman & Associates.

For another example, Jim Caforio was Terri's mentor and speech coach during her junior and senior years in high school. Now, 15 years down the road, that two-year span is relatively insignificant. Although Jim's pearls of wisdom remain firmly in her mind, she no longer approaches him for validation of her ideas and projects. It was a short-term mentoring relationship.

GROUP MENTORING

Floyd has helped to develop the concept of group mentoring, which is being undertaken by a number of students from his training programs. The group mentoring concept is being approached in different ways by several different groups, but the underlying themes are self-discipline and longevity. The groups tend to limit the size of their membership and set qualifications for who can join them. Unlike the typical business support group, which generally has people leaving and joining almost continuously, group mentoring programs tend to be closed to new members once they are formed. The reason for this is so the group can progress with a defined set of goals as a single unit and not be slowed or distracted by the influence of new members who are not up to speed. Other groups have strict prerequisite requirements pertaining to industry-specific training courses the prospective member must take before being considered for membership. The group assigns projects that members must complete on their own time. Many of these involve written reports and presentations that pertain to long-term planning. Some members of the mentoring groups drive from across the state, hundreds of miles, to meet with their group, usually on a monthly basis.

An interesting new twist on Floyd's group mentoring was shared by one young man who called us after hearing about our plans to write this book. He told us what he and several friends are doing along the lines of mentoring to help them keep to their goals.

First they developed a list of people whom they respected and decreed that they be their own personal board of directors. This is without talking to them or getting their permission, mind you. Then they sent everyone on the list a letter with a list of their personal goals and asked them for help. While these people weren't necessarily mentors, they served as the team's system of checks and balances in keeping them accountable to their goals.

The individuals on the list were friends and acquaintances whom they talked to from time to time. The young man reports that whenever they now talk with one of these people, it never fails that sometime during the course of the conversation the person asks, "So have you hit your goal yet?" or "Are you getting closer to your goal?" It's as if their goals never die because all these people are now constantly checking on them to see if they followed through and completed their objectives.

"We just sent them the list and told them what we were committing to and said, 'As a friend, I want to tell you what I am doing. Feel free to ask me whether or not I've hit my goals.'"

It's a great idea—not really group mentoring, but interesting! When we asked him why he did it, the young man explained: "It makes you commit to your goals by telling other people what you intend to do." *You don't back down, back out, give up, or blow your goals off as easily once you have told people whom you respect what you intend to do.* If you falter, you lose credibility.

MOMENTARY MENTORS

The last type of mentor is a momentary mentor, a person who pops into your life, gives you a pearl of wisdom, and then is gone. They are obviously not long-term mentors, but neither are they short-term mentors. They are people who make you stop and think for a moment—maybe longer, maybe forever.

A story shared with us by motivational speaker and investment counselor Rhoda Israelov illustrates how a momentary mentor can change your life.

USING MEDIA TO GET THAT ONE GREAT IDEA

It was December 1, 1983, and as I rode in my colleague Michael's car to the tax shelter seminar to be held that weekend at the Dayton Airport Inn, I was all but resolved to leave the investment sales field, accepting myself as a failure. Despite the encouragement of Michael and our other traveling companion and colleague, Robert, I could not shake my despondency. My closing rate on investment sales was not sufficient to clear business expenses and take care of my needs and those of the three sons I was raising on my own after the divorce. I felt I had run harder and faster than anyone in the office, and yet, somehow, it wasn't working. In my own mind, I envisioned the seminar as a last ditch effort to rekindle my enthusiasm or as my farewell meeting.

During the day and a half of jovial meals, hearty sales talk, and promises of wonderful investment results through investing in real estate, cable television, and other limited partnerships, I remained emotionally aloof and rather cynical, with a "yeah, yeah . . ." attitude. The sessions dragged on until finally it was time for the long drive home.

continues

---

concluded

As we left the hotel, we noticed that a thick fog had all but obscured the automobiles in the parking lot, but, after a hasty conference, we decided to make the trip. Michael climbed into the driver's seat with Robert at his side. Tired and depressed, I lay down in the back seat. Michael suggested we pass the time by listening to a set of Denis Waitley motivational tapes he had just received and which he had not yet had the time to enjoy.

For the next three hours, as the car crept through the fog, we were silent, with Denis Waitley's resonant voice the only one we heard. At first I was apathetic, but slowly began to heed the words on the tape and the hope they described of effecting a change in my life. Denis suggested finding one specific project and concentrating all one's effort on it for one month, without worrying about success or failure.

I remembered that the one investment I had liked of those presented at the seminar was a cable television partnership. What if I concentrated only on selling that one investment to people, all through the month of December? Could it work for me the way the voice on the tape was describing? By the time we arrived in Indianapolis, I was firmly resolved to give it a do-or-die try. If nothing else, I'd go out in flames, I thought.

So, for every day in the month of December—days, nights, weekends—I talked about the cable television industry and about this partnership. On New Year's Eve, I was still selling, I was so excited! Needless to say, I had an excellent commission month in January, due to all the business and all the excitement I had generated, in myself as well as in my clients.

Two happy endings mark this story. First, six years after my sale of cable television partnerships, the partnerships were sold and six times the invested capital was returned to my investors, one of the most successful investments they had ever made! Second, having totally forgotten about my resolve to quit the business, I went on to become the first female vice-president of E. F. Hutton in Indiana and to achieve several advanced degrees in financial planning.

A great Jewish teacher and philosopher, Maimonides, said that charity comes in degrees of greatness, with the greatest charity of all being a situation in which the donor and the recipient do not know one another. It is a momentary mentor who leaves a priceless gift. Even a momentary mentor can change your life.

POSSIBLE AREAS FOR MENTORING

Let's now take a closer look at a few common areas that you might consider appropriate for mentoring. Some of these will be very recognizable, and others you probably would never have considered when you think of how a mentor can further your goals.

A list of possible areas where you might consider having a mentor help you—or serving as a mentor to someone else—includes the following:

- ❖ Career and professional
- ❖ Family
- ❖ Spiritual
- ❖ Health/fitness/athletics
- ❖ Educational
- ❖ Social graces/protocol
- ❖ Philanthropic
- ❖ Ethical
- ❖ Financial

Career and Professional

Of course the professional arena is one of the most common areas for mentoring. Having a mentor guide you while you advance along your career is one of the more traditional applications of the concept. You might start by identifying someone who has achieved success in the area in which you want to excel or by finding someone who is successful in an area where you need improvement. Once you have your specific goal in mind, you can ask somebody who has already attained a certain level or position. If you work in a corporation, you might want to have three or four mentors in different areas who help you with the technical aspects of the business, with the managerial side, and perhaps with financial decisions.

Mentors for Family Matters

Having a mentor to answer questions about and help you with family matters is in certain cultures a time-honored tradition. Imagine that you are planning to start a family, but you have no idea what you are getting into. You might want to approach a relative or member of your church who has what you consider to be a model family. Ask what their difficulties have been and what pearls of wisdom they can share that have kept the family healthy and growing. There is no rule book, no fixed plan on how to raise a successful and loving family—there are too many variables.

Find one or several families you think would make good role models and get to know them. Tell them you want to be as successful in raising your family as they have been with theirs and ask them straight out if they would coach you occasionally. Tell them that you want to be a better parent or a better spouse.

Spiritual

Many times we get lost along life's path or we have questions or doubts about our own spirituality. It is a good idea to be able to consult with someone who has had similar fears and doubts or someone who shows great strength in their beliefs. It could be your minister, pastor, or rabbi, or someone else who is very strong in their beliefs. Your resolve and ability to overcome life's difficulties will be enhanced by the experience this person can share based on the challenges they have overcome in years past.

Health and Fitness

There are many times when you need encouragement just to keep fit. It's too easy to get lazy when you don't have any physical fitness goals. You might want to have your own professional coach—somebody who designs a plan that works for you. Many people have been helped by a fitness doctor. In terms of athletics, you want to find a coach who can help you perform at the level you dream of achieving. Aspiring Olympic heptathlon athlete Ali McKnight has five separate coaches for the seven sports she is training for—100-meter hurdles, high jump, shot put, 200 meters, long jump, javelin, and 800 meters. Several of the coaches are from various schools in the Long Beach, California, area, and none of them charges her or the other athletes for their time. "They help us as part of a volunteer effort in support of the Olympics," McKnight says. Without them, she could never have reached the world-class level at which she performs.

Educational

Oftentimes the key to success is getting the right kind of education. But there are an infinite number of programs and hundreds of different colleges. What program is right for the field you want to enter? Will you study under the right professors? Will you make the right contacts? Many times schools have counselors who are trained to help students with these types of questions. But another approach is to find someone who is doing what you want to do and ask: Where did you go to school? What classes did you take? If you could change your educational choices in any way, what would you have done differently? Are there any particular teachers/professors you might suggest I meet with to discuss my goals and plans? These kinds of questions will provide the initial answers you need to move forward with your plans toward your personal goals.

Social Graces

Regardless of how hard we work to improve our skills at work, we might find that we wind up being held back by our social skills— or lack of them. A mentor to help us polish our manners and speech could be the most important friend we ever had.

We can't help but think of the long-running Broadway musical hit and movie, *My Fair Lady*, based on George Bernard Shaw's play, *Pygmalion*. This story is about a professor so convinced he could teach anybody manners that, on a bet, he recruits from the streets of London a cockney wench with a nasty accent and horrible habits and trains her to be a paragon of high society. He shows her how to talk, walk, eat, and dance, what social events to attend, what to say, and what not to say. Finally she turns into a real lady and she doesn't need him anymore. She leaves him, but by then he is already in love with her. He ends up learning a valuable lesson—that nobody owes you something just because you help them improve themselves. The story also shows how you can elevate yourself in society if someone is willing to teach you the proper social graces.

Philanthropic

Helping any number of worthy social causes is a great way to contribute to the community or nation. Besides improving the region where you live, it gives you a sense of belonging and generally makes you feel good about yourself. Philanthropy is one of the characteristics we have found over and over among successful people. It raises the question: If you start giving, will you be successful? Can you achieve the results of successful people by patterning your behavior on theirs, even though it may not seem to relate directly to your goal? In our opinion, the answer is a resounding yes. It is difficult to cite exactly why this works, but the evidence is overwhelming that it does. Getting involved in organizations that need our time, talents, and support is something we all need to do if we are serious about success. But once you have decided to get involved, don't you need some help in deciding where and how to devote your time and energies? This is an appropriate area for someone to serve as your mentor, or, if you are already involved, to encourage and support a newcomer.

Ethical

One of the most challenging areas for people today—particularly successful people—is to determine what is ethical and fair in the increasingly complicated and "politically correct" society in which we live. What is acceptable today may be offensive tomorrow. A mentor who has experience in these areas can provide insight that can save us much grief, not to mention nasty and often unnecessary lawsuits. All we have to do to see how big a problem this really is today is look at the egregious failures of the many high-profile people who are written up in the daily newspaper. The exploits of the British royal family have been the fodder for the world's tabloids for more than several years. Who was giving them advice? None of us wants to wind up in unpleasant situations. Having a mentor to bounce ideas off of can prevent a lot of discomfort. Ethics mentors can help you establish your personal standards and beliefs and discuss areas that might be the most important criteria for a happy, healthy, and balanced life.

Financial

Usually if you are looking for someone to be a financial coach, you will be looking for somebody who is financially successful. You ask her how she started saving, or how she started to accumulate wealth.

You probably would be interested in where she makes her investments and why. It gets a little tricky sometimes when the field you are interested in requires a very high degree of specialization. If someone isn't a professional financial counselor, you might be concerned whether she really knows what she is talking about before you put your money into a recommended investment. You may also need to seek professional guidance. Whether you seek a mentor or a professional consultant, it has to be someone you believe in. One group of women investors in the Midwest became widely known after their investment club started scoring big successes in the stock market. They formed a group, the Beardstown Ladies, to advise and mentor each other, and the results exceeded what many mutual funds with professional managers achieved. Again, the power of synergy in mentoring exceeds what an individual can do on his or her own.

Emotional

Emotional mentoring is perhaps one of the most common in existence. Most people have a friend or soul mate upon whom they can call to pour out their hearts. If you don't have someone like this, and you can afford it, you might seek a professional counselor. There are also many free services that you can call upon through your church or other organizations. Having an emotional mentor is a great idea, and using the techniques in this book to find the right person who can give you sound, balanced advice is definitely a way to go. There are a lot of people who are willing to be mentors in this area. Be selective in your choice of mentors. You want good advice from someone who has his or her life together.

MENTORING ENHANCES OTHER TYPES OF TRAINING

We want to emphasize that mentoring does not replace other types of training, it enhances it. We are not saying that in all these areas your mentor is the final word on the subject. Your mentor is a sounding board and a source of pearls of wisdom. You still need to read continuously. If you have a mentor for family issues, you may still need to go to seminars or classes on family development. Similarly, in the life's other major areas, such as finance, health and fitness, spirituality, and social graces, you may need to take classes, consult newspapers and magazines, dive into books, and go to discussion groups. Use your mentor as a springboard to finding the most effective help available.

If we want to achieve success in a given area, we need every single tool available to us. That means computer technology, literature, videotapes, college classes, counseling, newspapers, magazines, trade show publications, brainstorming groups, everything. Having a mentor is similar to having a coach to help you work with these tools more effectively.

Mentors are not the solution to every problem. Sometimes you need to obtain professional advice, which you must pay for! Mentors are not paid for their services, and there are times when it's very appropriate to pay for someone's help. For one thing, when you pay for an expert to solve a problem for you, that person has ownership of the problem until it is resolved. A mentor has much less responsibility—and liability! A mentor is someone who can help you solve your problem yourself. However, we don't always want a do-it-yourself solution. Sometimes we want an expert to just take care of the problem.

Some good advice from mentors has been simply, "Hire a good attorney. This is not my area of specialization." A mentor sometimes is the place to go to for counseling on where to find experts. You don't look for a mentor to do your bookkeeping—you pay an accountant. A mentor is not an attorney to take care of your legal problems, mentors provide a different kind of service.

Nevertheless, mentoring has an important role in everyday life. The world today is crying for help, and ignorance continues to be the basis for many decisions. The authors believe that if each of us had a mentor, and each of us had a protégé, then the world would be vastly improved. People today need to leave their comfort zone and learn to adapt to change. Mentors help us venture out; they make it a little bit easier, a little bit more palatable to undergo dramatic change. You have your own personal coach to help you get over the bumps.

CHANGING TO MEET THE CHALLENGE

Many people may say, "I just can't change. And it's not my nature to ask someone else for help." Well, we are all human, and being able to change differentiates us from the animal kingdom. We can do it if we are sufficiently motivated. Some people, however, don't realize they have the capacity to change. Sometimes you can tell someone something time and again—find a mentor, do your homework, whatever—but he or she doesn't hear you. It reminds us of the famous story about the frog and the scorpion.

A frog is swimming in a pond, and a scorpion saddles up to the shore and says, "Hey, Mr. Frog, I really would like to get over to the other side of the pond. Will you let me jump on your back while we swim across?"

"No way!," says the frog. "You will sting me."

"Why would I do that?" asks the scorpion. "That would be stupid. We would both drown!"

"I guess you're right," the frog says. "OK, hop on."

The frog starts swimming across the pond, but about half-way across he feels an incredible pain in his back. His muscles start going numb, and he can't move his legs.

"What in the world was that?," asks the frog incredulously. "Are you some kind of an idiot? You stung me!"

"Yes," says the scorpion mournfully.

"But why?" asks the frog. "Now we're both going to die!"

"I couldn't help it," says the scorpion. "It's just my nature."

Often we see people who start a relationship or a project and then sabotage it. It just seems to be their nature. If you want to succeed, you will have to break out of bad, but sometimes familiar, habits.

The scorpion couldn't break his own habit. That's half the battle in achieving success. People often can't muster the humility to be able to take somebody else's advice and do something a little different from what their instincts tell them. Just because a pattern or a process exists doesn't mean it can't be rearranged a little to achieve a higher level of success and happiness. Use the mentoring process as an instrument for change and avoid sabotaging yourself by repeating learned, but outdated behavior.

Ultimately, as in most areas of life, *what we get out of mentoring is what we put into it*. If we make a commitment to adopt a mentoring lifestyle, we will see some remarkable changes begin to take place. How we relate to the world will begin to change little by little, day by day. Life will begin to be a little more enjoyable, a little more productive. However, creating and maintaining a mentoring relationship takes commitment and work both on the part of the protégé and the mentor. The mentor's investment in time and emotion can be significant, and there are risks involved, so it is not to be undertaken lightly. For the mentor, the rewards are usually deferred for some time. For the protégé, there is a more immediate payback, but there is more work as well. After all, it is up to the protégé to follow through on the tasks assigned by the mentor.

FORMER PROTÉGÉS ARE THE MOST ENTHUSIASTIC MENTORS

Research has found that, not surprisingly, the most enthusiastic mentors are people who earned their stripes as protégés some time earlier. If you have been a protégé to someone else, you understand the benefits. Isn't it time you begin to give back some of what you have been given to advance your life to where it is today? If you are a protégé, consider screening your potential mentors for whether they were protégés during some earlier period. Your request for support may be met with more enthusiasm from a former protégé than from someone completely unfamiliar with the process.

We have now shown you the six basic types of mentoring relationships and how one or all of these might help you in specific areas of your life, whether it be financial, ethical, emotional, or other areas where you want to progress. The point is that, if you want to be successful, mentoring in a broad range of areas can help you realize your dreams and make your life more fulfilling. You can adapt mentoring to be what you want it to be and customize your relationships to meet your personal needs and circumstances. We also emphasized that mentoring isn't a substitute for a professional when you need highly specific information or a skilled service. But it is a way for us to cope with the many changes facing us today in our careers and personal lives for which we might not otherwise be prepared.

In the next chapter, we will discuss the specific benefits of becoming both a mentor and a protégé and explain in more detail why you should invest your time in this way. We also will discuss the qualifications you should have in order to fulfill either role successfully, so you can decide if mentoring is for you. Just to make sure you have the proper tools to get started when you do decide to give mentoring a try, we will show you what to do and say to find either a mentor or a protégé, and how to evaluate someone to serve in that role.

HIGHLIGHTS

❖ There are seven basic types of mentoring: primary, secondary, structured versus informal, active versus passive, long-term versus short-term, group, and momentary.

❖ The most important mentor is your primary mentor—the person you talk to about a broad variety of questions.

❖ A secondary mentor is someone we go to for specific areas of interest. We recommend having one primary mentor and several secondary mentors.

❖ A structured mentor program is one with a set protocol and list of rules. An informal mentor relationship can be very productive, but it lacks the clear guidelines.

❖ An active mentor is someone who is routinely available to the protégé. A passive mentor may help someone who is less experienced on an occasional basis. Passive mentors may be found in abundance through their works in the library.

❖ Long-term mentors may be available for years, but they don't necessarily have to be the protégé's primary mentor.

❖ Group mentoring differs from typical support group associations in that the groups are often closed to new members.

❖ A twist on group mentoring is the "personal board of directors," a set of people to whom you have formally announced your goals.

❖ Momentary mentors may change your life, though you may see them but once.

❖ Different areas for mentoring are almost innumerable and include career, family, spiritual, health, education, etiquette, philanthropy, and ethics, among others.

CHAPTER

The Benefits of Having a Mentor, and How to Select One

You become as your teacher, therefore, select with care.
Mary Rudisill

In the last chapter, we covered the many different types of mentors and we discussed specific areas where you might want to consider improving your abilities through the help of a mentor who has experience in those areas. In this chapter, we will outline just how you can benefit by having a mentor and describe the behavior you should exhibit toward your mentor. Then we show you exactly how to go about finding a mentor. While some of our more knowledgeable and experienced readers might think they are beyond serving as a protege, our philosophy is that everyone remains on life's road to self-improvement and self-fulfillment until the end of his or her days. In short, you are never too old to be a protege. No matter your stage of life, you will continue to have goals and need help adapting to constant change. A mentor can help you do that.

WHAT CAN I EXPECT FROM A MENTORING RELATIONSHIP?

We are somewhat amused when an individual wants to learn to be a top performer in an industry and he wants to be paid to learn it.

A mentoring relationship is very similar to an internship. When you perform in an internship position, you work like a dog, and either you don't get paid or you get paid very little. In many internships you might work from 9 to 5 for a company or organization and never get paid a dime. That's because they are giving you the information and passing along the knowledge you need to go out and create a better opportunity for yourself. Nobody should pay you to learn. You have to be willing, hungry, and assertive. The first principle is that if you don't care enough to enrich yourself through your education, knowledge, and experience then you probably aren't going to get very far. Those people who always have a hand outstretched imploring, "Give me!" could be waiting a long time, especially in today's competitive environment.

There has to be a commitment to self-improvement on the part of the protege. When Terri was speaking not long ago at the Constitutional Rights Foundation Youth Business Conference in Irvine, California, her topic was how to find a mentor. While delivering this talk to some 600 students, an interesting aspect of human behavior revealed itself. While offering to help put students in touch with someone in their chosen career field, she uncovered a pervasive attitude of passiveness.

EARNING YOUR OWN OPPORTUNITIES

While speaking to this group of young people, I thought they would appreciate an offer to connect with someone in a field they were considering as a career choice. I told them, "Through my group of associates, we can introduce you to someone who is involved with the profession you would like to enter after you graduate. If you would like me to help you find a mentor at this point, I would be happy to do so. All you have to do is write a letter telling me what field you want to enter, and I will do my best to help you obtain your first appointment."

One young fellow stood up at the back of the room and asked, "What are you going to pay me to write you this letter?"

"What am I going to pay you?" I asked incredulously. "Why should I pay you to help you build your own dream?"

He said, "Yeah, it takes a lot of time, you know, to sit down and write this letter and put all this stuff together. And what am I going to do—work for this person for free?"

continues

---

continued

I was in shock. I shouldn't have been because many adults I know are surprised at the suggestion they can get ahead by working with a mentor. Most people never reach their goals because they are too afraid to invest their time and energy without a guarantee of a return on their investment. And this young man wasn't about to make a fool of himself by doing anything that didn't guarantee instant gratification. He just didn't get it. I was now looking at a room full of kids, and they all were waiting to see if I were going to pay the one who had enough courage to speak up. So I said, "Well, that's an interesting point. Let me ask everyone in this room. What if I told you that I would give you $500 to write the letter, as long as you got it to me by next Friday. How many of you would do it?" The whole room put up their hands.

"What if I said, oops, I overestimated. There are too many people in this room, and I really don't have that kind of money. What if I drop my offer to $100? Now, how many would do it?" Only half of them raised their hands. "What if I said I'm not willing to pay you anything to write the letter—how many of you would do it anyway?"

About 10 students held up their hands. I was very surprised, but I shouldn't have been. I realize now it was typical. Most people, including young people, are somewhat cynical about jumping at someone else's proposition. They want proof before they invest any of their precious time in something. It goes deeper than their just being busy, however. It is the manifestation of what I call the "employee mentality" whereby a person is unwilling to try anything unless someone pays him or her for it.

In spite of my disappointment with the response, I kept my composure, and said, "This is a very special moment in your lives, ladies and gentlemen. What you are about to learn is that nobody is going to pay you to realize your dreams. The only person who will benefit by your putting forth the effort required to find a mentor is you.

"Once you realize you are never going to get ahead by doing the minimum, you will welcome the opportunity to perform extra tasks—such as writing letters—as a way to better yourself. When you recognize that doing the minimum will ensure minimum results, you will commit yourself to looking for opportunities that result in personal growth, not immediate financial benefit. And, if you are lucky enough, someone might take the time to mentor you. If you are fortunate enough to be blessed by someone more knowl-

continues

---

concluded

edgeable than yourself spending time with you, the result will be an immediate shortcut to realizing your dreams. But you are going to have to earn that advantage through hard work. For the same reason I'm not going to pay you to write a letter to find a mentor, nobody is going to pay you to create opportunities for yourself in life. You are going to have to work and earn them."

What is really frightening is that these young people are representative of the population at large. There seems to be a widespread belief in our society that somehow, someone is supposed to pay us to do the work to make our dreams come true. The fact is, it's not going to happen.

At this point, it should be clear what the benefits are of being a protege. They are endless. But just to enumerate a few of the foremost, we will list nine of the most important. Mentors can:

1. Open doors
2. Provide coaching and advice on setting goals
3. Save you time
4. Save you money
5. Reduce your frustration
6. Increase your success and productivity
7. Improve your career satisfaction
8. Enhance your overall sense of well being
9. Increase your levels of commitment and loyalty

1. Opening Doors

Regardless of how hard you had to work to get a mentor to commit to help you, once you have that commitment in hand, a mentor will begin opening doors for you, doors you could not have opened by yourself. You will have increased social interaction and networking with others in your desired profession or field. This means contacts, other potential mentors and associates, and perhaps even job opportunities. This is going to make life *a lot* easier. You will have to perform to your mentor's standards, but he or she will create opportunities you couldn't have made for yourself. And if you did it by yourself it would have taken a lot more effort.

2. Providing Coaching and Advice on Setting Goals

Mentors provide the coaching, goal-setting, advice, and troubleshooting that ultimately will save you time, money, and sanity and provide better personal security.

3. Saving You Time

You will save time because your mentor has already "been there and done that." If you were going to try to learn the same things through personal experience, it would take you far more time and create a few headaches along the way. So why not learn through their experiences?

4. Saving You Money

One of the things we always do is ask people, what is your time worth? Someone usually says something like, "I get paid $15 an hour."

"OK, so your time is worth $15 an hour?" The person says, "Right."

"So if you spend 10 hours building your dream, that is going to cost you $150, right?" And the individual says, "Right."

"But if you were going to meet with a mentor who gave you the pearls of wisdom to transform 10 hours of work on your dream down to only three hours with the same results, you have basically just saved yourself $105." And some people's time is worth far more.

Having a mentor can help you earn money over the long term because a mentor can put you on a fast track to increasing your income. You will have the strategic coaching and improved opportunities to better position yourself down the road.

5. Reducing Frustration

In the long run, this saves your sanity. In an attempt to conserve money, some people will create great stress in their personal lives by doing everything by themselves. A mentor alleviates some of that intense aloneness and provides coaching. When you are on your own you might experience super highs and super lows. It is this emotional rollercoaster that makes people just give up or stop trying so hard. A mentor puts you on a more balanced path. It is easier to live with change when you have a more even-keeled approach and perspective. And a mentor gives you more personal security while you are en route to paying your dues.

6. Increasing Your Success and Productivity

A colleague of ours was a protege to a very successful computer software industry executive. He was her manager at work, but they would meet afterwards and talk. They stayed in touch even after he left the company, and he continued to give her advice. Finally, he said, "You know, it might be a good time for you to move on to another firm. I think you are ready to go after a new opportunity."

She started interviewing and was able to offer a whole new set of skills based on the information she had learned from her mentor. She went from a job that earned $50,000 a year base to $70,000 a year plus commissions. Mentors most definitely can help you enhance your opportunities and earning capacity.

7. Improving Your Career Satisfaction

A mentor can contribute to the satisfaction you get from your career or even a simple goal. When someone else is there to see you through all your struggles, helps you when you stumble, and is there to cheer for you at the awards ceremony when you accomplish a goal, you can take greater satisfaction in your success.

8. Enhancing Your Overall Sense of Well-Being

A mentor can also help keep you moving forward. There is an old saying that if you aren't moving forward you are going backward. Mentors keep you thinking and moving in a forward direction. When you are constantly striving to reach the next level, you can accomplish more than you ever imagined and, naturally, you get a lot more personal satisfaction and your overall sense of well-being is enhanced.

9. Increasing Your Levels of Commitment and Loyalty

If you are happy and satisfied and have a sense of well-being within your environment, then naturally your commitment and loyalty to your current organization increases. If you are satisfied with your present situation and find it comfortable and productive, you will become increasingly loyal. You will value that empowering opportunity, and it will be easier to stay.

Often people say, I could never stay in a job for 10 years, or I could never do this kind of work for 25 years (like my father did). It seems many people today see their jobs as being so restrictive to their careers that, when asked, they will say something like, "I'll do this for a couple of years, and then I'll leave."

Are people anticipating boredom to set in at exactly the 24-month point? Is this likely? If you were in an environment where all of your needs were being met, and your career had direction—as attested to by your mentor—then your loyalty and commitment could very well be enough to prevent your feeling so infernally restless. It might be easier to stay and build on the opportunities where you are.

We all want to work with people who are loyal and committed. Employers seeking new recruits are also looking for these characteristics. Is there an unwritten canon that says you have to leave a company after two years? Since there is generally pain with separation, why not create an environment where there is no need to separate from a group that has the potential to meet your needs? If you have the ability, through your relationships with mentors, to bring resources into the group instead of searching outside the group to meet your needs, both you and your employer can benefit.

The following story by Debbie Bermont of St. Louis, Missouri-based Source Communications illustrates how much impact a mentor can have on your life, relating to the benefits we described above.

OVERCOMING YOUTHFUL IMPATIENCE

When I first met my mentor he was walking around the office in large, fuzzy, bear slippers. Perhaps this was his source of creative

continues

continued

energy. In any case, it should have been an immediate and clear indication to me about his personality. I had responded to an ad for an assistant in a marketing agency. Fresh out of college, I was bold, confident, eager to learn, and willing to take any position to break into the field of marketing and advertising. This was my shot.

What I didn't know when I took the position was how much my boss would influence my life. I wasn't particularly looking for a mentor. Until the past few years as my understanding of the world has changed and my awareness about people expanded, I didn't know I even needed a mentor. As I continue to grow and learn and share my wisdom, I am ever more grateful for the people who have contributed significantly to my life. The man was much more than my boss—he became my mentor.

So if you can picture meeting a man who starts his day at 4 a.m., who thinks sleep is an inconvenience, who wears fuzzy slippers, who has more energy than a basketball team, who has traveled the world many times over, who drives a Harley Davidson motorcycle, who is a well-respected author, consultant, and speaker and who has a tremendous heart, then you will know and love Ray Jutkins, or, as he is known in the direct marketing community, "Rocket" Ray Jutkins.

Mentors aren't just teachers, they are people who motivate you to change your life. This may be conscious or unconscious. When I first started working for Ray in 1983, I didn't know that he would change my life so significantly. He was the partner in a direct marketing agency with over 20 years of marketing experience. Ray was a consummate salesman, selling clients on the marketing programs appropriate to companies. I worked with Ray to fulfill his promises to his clients. When he promised to produce something for our client, I made it happen.

The toughest part of this position was when he would promise something I felt was unrealistic. That left me to figure out how to do it. Ray taught me there were no problems, only opportunities. Ray did not understand what the word "no" meant so I was encouraged to be flexible and use creative thinking.

The best part of Ray's management style was that he would hand me the reigns to drive the coach, but always kept a watchful eye that I didn't steer the wagon in the wrong direction. On one occasion, when I was particularly persistent in my request for career advancement, Ray taught me the most valuable lesson about impatience I

continues

---

concluded

would ever learn. He told me I was a lot sharper than most people. He said that having drive and being a little impatient was good, but I must learn to trust that things will happen when they are meant to happen. To a 24-year-old, this made no sense. To a 34-year-old, it makes perfect sense.

As a mentor, Ray went beyond just being a good boss. He instilled confidence so I could achieve anything I wanted to do. He showed me that there really are no boundaries to life. He is a passionate person, and he allowed me to share in his passion for excellence and recognition.

After four years, Ray left the agency and started his own professional speaking and consulting business. Through the years, there have been many occasions when I have actively sought Ray's advice. He has unselfishly given me words of wisdom that always hold true. He has sent me articles, notes of support, and information that have helped me enormously in my professional career.

Just recently I saw Ray at a national conference. As I was telling him about my current clients and efforts to generate new business, once again he reminded me about the lesson on impatience. Impatience is good, but trust things to happen when they are meant to happen. It is this trust that is now the foundation of my belief system, which has led to my success.

I don't know if Ray stills walks around in fuzzy bear slippers, but I do know I am truly blessed for having him as a mentor in my life.

Having a good mentor can affect not only your outlook, but your whole life. The benefits go way beyond the few we have listed. In order to attract a good mentor, however, you must be the type of person someone would want to take on as a protege. Let's now look at the qualities you should possess in order to be a suitable protege candidate.

QUALIFICATIONS OF A GOOD PROTÉGÉ

There are four basic traits that we have found to be present in most protégés who are successful in a mentoring relationship. It is somewhat obvious why. Protégés who value and respect their mentor's time and advice naturally are going to be more appealing to a mentor. A successful protégé:

❖ Respects the mentor's time.

❖ Takes action on information provided by the mentor.

❖ Shows respect for the mentor's efforts to open new doors.

❖ Passes on the gift of mentoring by taking on a protégé.

Respect Your Mentor's Time

The first requirement or qualification for being a protégé is to respect your mentor's time. If your time is worth $15 an hour, your mentor's time may be worth $100 an hour. You have to recognize and respect the fact this person is making a bigger investment in this relationship initially than you are. In addition to the measurable cost of the mentor's time, there is little return for him or her at the startup of the relationship. The mentor might not get any return from you for a year down the road until he or she sees that the investment has paid off. Therefore it is critically important that you respect his or her time.

Take Action on the Information Provided by Your Mentor

You must also take action on the information that your mentor provides to you. There are few things worse for a mentor than for him or her to give you a list of things to do and have you fail to follow up. You get together for your next meeting, and your mentor asks, "What did you do with the things I told you to do?," You respond, "Well, I didn't really get to them—I wanted to, but . . ."

The response is going to be, "Forget it! I'm not going to give you any more advice. You didn't even follow up on the advice I gave you the first time. Why should I give you any more?" Suddenly, that magic of mentoring is nipped in the bud. You have to *earn the right* to hear the secrets of the masters. The way you do that is by taking action on the tasks they give you. If you don't follow up on the assignments, then you don't earn the right to hear the next—and more advanced—secret.

You have to perform the basic steps to get to the next secret. And you have to follow up on the next set of steps to get to the even bigger secrets. This goes on until you evolve into someone with whom mentors are going to share their most precious pearls of wisdom—pearls that you need to know in order to reach your goal, pearls of immeasurable value.

If you don't build your relationship by taking action, you also hurt yourself because you lengthen the time it's going to take to learn the secrets that mentors have to share. They won't tell you until they feel you are prepared to hear.

Show Respect for Your Mentor's Efforts

The next requirement is for you to go through the doors your mentor opens for you. You do this remembering to honor and respect your mentor's efforts. Your behavior and follow-through with people to whom he or she might introduce you is how you express that respect.

For instance, you want to dress appropriately and be polished and articulate when you meet with a mentor's contacts. You only have the chance to go through these doors because of your mentor, so respect the opportunities he or she has provided you.

Pass on the Gift of Mentoring

The protégé must be willing to pass on the gift of mentoring by in turn mentoring someone else. In the long run, after someone has made an investment in you, you can return the favor by making a similar investment in some other worthy protégé seeking help.

Once you have determined that you possess all four qualifications of a successful protégé, you will begin considering how to actually go about the process of approaching potential mentors.

SELECTING YOUR MENTOR

Say you are at the point now where you say, OK, I think I've got it. I understand nobody is going to pay me to make my dreams come true. I know that in order to be a protégé I have to earn the right, and there are certain qualifications I must have. I know I have to be committed before I can ask someone to be my mentor. I'm going to respect my mentor's time. I'm willing to take action on the information he or she provides. I will take the initiative to pass through the doors my mentor opens for me, and I will honor any position offered me. I am also committed to passing on the gift of mentor-

ing by being a mentor to someone else when that opportunity aris-
es. So, I'm ready to become a protégé, but how do I find, select, and
begin working with a mentor? For many people, finding a mentor
can be one of the most difficult tasks. It really takes commitment.

The following story from a friend and colleague, whom we
will call Lynn, shows how the average person can achieve above-
average results—and realize their dreams—through the help of a
mentor who has been selected *proactively*.

CREATING THAT FIRST BIG BREAK

Throughout my education, and even afterward in my career, I was
fortunate enough to meet people who were willing to serve as mentors. I had always networked with people in my organization, looking for truisms and help along the way.

The time came when I wanted to branch out and become
involved in acting, film, and television. I wasn't sure what to do. At
first I did the traditional things that people said I should—meet with
a photographer, get photos of myself, and visit the various agencies
in hopes of having one represent me.

It took a long time, but after sending for a list of agents from the
Screen Actors Guild, the precious names finally arrived in the mail.
I dutifully called each one, but they all said the same thing: Send us
your pictures and don't call us, we'll call you. After playing this
game for about six months, I got very frustrated. Finally I realized—
this just wasn't working.

My next approach was to make a second round of calls to the Screen
Actors Guild agencies in my local area. I asked if I could meet with the
director of each agency one on one. Only two out of about 20 agreed
to meet with me for a personal interview. Only one of those two was
interested in carrying me. I soon found out, however, that just because
they sign you to the agency doesn't mean you will get any work. So
after another four months of never once being sent out for an audition,
I really started to wonder if this is what I should be doing.

Next I decided I would commit to reading all the trade publications in the field. I went to the library to research what magazines
and trade groups were out there, and I went back to my college professors and to ask them if they had any suggestions. I learned about

continues

concluded

an organization specifically for television producers and executives. I made it my goal to become a member of that group. I realized that if all the other organizations were made up of actors and actresses, they really couldn't help me. The people I wanted to talk to were the producers and executives.

Traveling in these circles costs money, and I began saving to pay for the membership fee. I started getting the group's newsletter and learned they were planning an annual national meeting. This too would be expensive. I saved up enough money to pay for the registration, flight, and hotel accommodations. Scared, but armed with my photos and my resume (which basically had nothing on it) I made it to the conference.

The objective was to meet with as many people as I could. I began introducing myself and told them who I was. I went up to them in the trade show at the booths and to ones who were milling around—I even would start conversations in the cafeteria line just to get acquainted. All the attendees had name badges, so I would look at their tags to see what companies they were with, or what industry, or profession, then I would ask them about themselves.

During the course of three days, I met about 200 people. Of that group, exactly three took a genuine interest in me. Two of those three really couldn't help me on a personal level. They *were* very helpful, however, in finding other places I could go to find a mentor and learn more about the industry. One person—out of the entire 200—agreed to meet with me after the conference. I took him to lunch, and we had a very interesting meeting. Using the Terri and Floyd 21-step approach [outlined on page 70] I was able to cultivate a mentoring relationship with this individual. Almost two years later, he is still an active mentor and has helped me obtain my first major part in a television show with a major network.

Where Do You Find a Mentor?

You may want to consider the various organizations that provide mentors to people who ask for them. These include groups such as the Small Business Administration's Service Corps of Retired Executives (SCORE), which has a list of people willing to help others, particularly those starting out in business. There are also mentoring programs in churches and community organizations, and, for young people, the Boys and Girls Clubs of America. "Virtual mentors" are a real help to a number of individuals. A contributor to this book, Dottie Walters, whose mentor is Ben Franklin, found him in the library. This is an excellent place to start your quest for self-improvement and a good place to find a mentor. The father of one of our staff members found a virtual mentor in Carl Jung, the famous psychologist. All your business associations provide terrific opportunities for networking, which, in turn, can provide mentor candidates.

THE 21 STEPS TO CHOOSING YOUR MENTOR

1. brainstorm desires
2. set goal
3. identify achievers
4. select top candidates
5. research backgrounds
6. set goals for meeting
7. write letter to mentor prospect
8. call to set appointment
9. prepare 10 questions
10. ask to hear life story
11. state goals, ask questions
12. ask for suggestions
13. trial close
14. send thank-you note, gift
15. evaluate information
16. take action on mentor suggestions
17. call mentor with activity results
18. evaluate prospect's response
19. request second appointment
20. propose a mentoring relationship
21. commit to 16 Laws of Mentoring (covered in Chapter 6)

We have identified 21 steps to obtaining your unique mentor. You can use this process to get the relationship going. It will give you a means of controlling who you choose as a mentor and the time it takes. After that, the relationship will evolve according to your individual needs and personalities. Here is our proven formula for how to get someone to agree to be your mentor.

Step 1: Brainstorm Your Desires

The first thing you will do is decide in which area of your life you want a mentor—professional, financial, spiritual, and so on. For this you will have to do a little dreaming. First imagine what you would like to accomplish with your life. Where do you see yourself in a year? Five years? 10 years? Ask yourself this: If I could do anything in the world I want to, what would it be? Begin by making a list of your most inspiring choices. Then you will need to focus on one main goal or objective and make your final choice.

Step 2: Set a Specific Goal

Perhaps you want to write a book. The first step is to commit to that book. What kind of book would it be? You have to break it down into detailed pieces. You might want to work in the television and media industry. Great, what do you want to do there? Do you want to be a broadcaster? What type? OK, you want to be a newscaster. What medium do you want to work in—television? Not radio, or newspapers? Now what kind of television newscaster do you want to be? Do you want to be a weather person, entertainment critic, or general news reporter? Do you want to travel around and do interviews like *Entertainment Tonight's* Leeza Gibbons? You have to hone in on the specific activity you want to be involved in. Now you identify the qualifications of someone who holds that position. Break them down into specific, identifiable parts. This will require a little research. Make a list of the qualifications of individuals who are doing what you would like to do.

Step 3: Identify the Achievers

Now ask yourself, who do I know and how do I identify individuals who have accomplished the goals I want to achieve? Then start making a list of all the people who have attained these goals. If you don't know anyone personally, which is entirely likely, start out at the library. Your local librarian can be a great resource in helping to find materials related to your specific goal. The library often will lead you to people, organizations, and associations related to your objectives. You might consider attending classes and asking your teachers and fellow classmates for referrals to other clubs and net-working groups that could lead you to finding a mentor. Here is a list of 12 common places to start your search for a mentor:

1. Local library
2. Career/placement services and counselors
3. Parents
4. Teachers
5. Colleges and associations
6. Trade journal editors
7. Networking groups
8. Professional associations
9. Service Corps of Retired Executives
10. Friends and family
11. The Internet
12. Church or spiritual family

As your search progresses, you will want to keep track of the names of people who hold promise as potential mentors. You need to be a little assertive. Pick up the phone and ask your friends and anyone you know if they can think of someone to whom they could refer you. The theory of "six degrees of separation" applies here— you are generally only six people away from finding someone you want to meet.

Once you have a list of the names of potential mentors, break it into three smaller lists divided geographically. You might have an A-list, B-list, and C-list. The A-list is comprised of people doing what you aspire to do on a nationwide scale. The B-list is people doing it statewide, and the C-list is local people. Naturally, it will be easier to access people on the C-list when you are just getting started. Accessibility is a big issue, because if you live in Los Angeles, and the heart surgeon you want for a mentor lives in Boston, you may have to move to Boston (or get active on the Internet.) The alternative, of course, is to pick someone accessible, someone in your own backyard. Having a mentor in another part of the country, however, is possible and in fact occurs frequently. For example, Terri lives in California, and Floyd lives in Michigan.

If you don't have a ready list of people yet to choose from, start by reviewing the above list of potential places to begin your search. Join associations that cater to the types of individuals you might consider to be suitable mentors. By networking and attending a few of these meetings, you will get an idea of who is available locally.

Step 4: Select Top Candidates

Next, sort through the list of potential mentors according to your knowledge of and respect for each. Try phoning a few to see if they might know of any associations or groups that have mentoring programs in your area of interest. Then sort the list also according to accessibility. Perhaps someone on your list is very well known. Let's say you want to be a doctor, specifically a heart surgeon. Perhaps there is someone very well known on your list, but you don't happen to like the way he works. Maybe he is ill-tempered or has a reputation of having trampled people on his way up the ladder of success. You don't want to be mentored by that type of person, so you just weed him out.

Step 5: Research Their Backgrounds

Begin your homework on the prospective mentors remaining on the list after the weeding-out process. Begin thinking about your goal of meeting with them. Say we want to write a business and professional book. We want it to be top quality and sell 50,000 copies. The first thing we do is begin looking for authors who have written business and professional books. Then we look for authors who have been published by large publishers. Next we look for those who have sold more than 50,000 copies of their books. Finally, we look for those who have met all these criteria—and live close to home! Where do you go to find them? Again, start with the basics. Use the library, get on the phone . . . be more than assertive—be tenacious. It's amazing what you can learn when you expend a little effort.

Obviously, you can't just walk up and knock on the door of someone in this league and tell her you want her to serve as your mentor. First, you must find out what, if anything, has been written by or about this person. Perhaps she has authored articles, or maybe her company has a media kit you can request. You are going to do a second weeding out after you complete your initial research, but first narrow the field a little so you don't have to do a lot of extra homework.

Step 6: Set Goals for Meetings

If you know specifically what you want to ask your prospective mentor and how you want to proceed, it is much easier to begin your approach. You are not merely calling him up to say, "Hi, let's be friends!" You have an agenda in mind, and you need to accomplish it. It will also help to put together a list of questions to take with you to the first meeting, as discussed below.

Steps 7 and 8: Write or Call to Set Appointment

Some people are going to be more approachable than others. Some of you will be able to simply call on the phone to set up an appointment. Perhaps you send a letter first, make a follow-up call, and, boom, they agree to meet with you. Other individuals are going to be more difficult to contact. Consider the advantages of actually meeting them first, then later sending them a letter.

If you wish to take this approach, begin by finding out the associations they belong to. Perhaps they are involved in the March of Dimes. Your approach then is to go to a few March of Dimes meetings—and network! Try to pursue some small-talk about a hobby of theirs or some other area of interest. After you have met them, spend a little time thinking about what you would like to communicate, then send a letter. Ask for an opportunity to meet with them, then wait a few days and make a follow-up call to set an appointment.

Step 9: Prepare 10 Questions

When you arrive, have 10 questions already prepared. These should be things you want to know in order to prepare yourself to reach your goal. Use your creativity when crafting these questions. You might ask: If you were where I am now, what would your next step be? When you were my age, what did you do at this particular crossroads in your life? What was your biggest mistake? If you could pass along a single pearl of wisdom, what would it be?

Propose a meeting wherever the mentor suggests. Usually, you will go to her office or a nearby restaurant. Make it as convenient as you can. Try to keep your initial meeting brief. Once you have met, the best way to break the ice is to get her to talk about herself. You don't want to start off by telling her about everything you have done up until this point in your life and how great you are— at least not until she has had an opportunity to talk a little about herself.

Step 10: Ask to Hear Their Life Story

One proven approach is to start the meeting by asking her to tell you her life story (keeping in mind, of course, how much time you have scheduled). Let her know how impressed you are by what she has accomplished. Tell her, "You have done so many of the things that I hope to accomplish someday, I was wondering if you can share your story with me. Tell me how you got started." There is an art to this form of persuasion, and it is executed through your delivery. You must sound polished and not as though you are trying to flatter her. Carry yourself well and have a warm demeanor so your potential mentor will feel comfortable sharing information.

Step 11: State Goals and Ask Questions

After the mentor tells you her life story, you should compliment her on the things she has accomplished. Once again, reinforce the idea that you would like to achieve some of the same goals and dreams she has. Say that you greatly appreciate her sharing her story with you. At this point, begin to define what you are interested in from the relationship. Share your background and your accomplishments at this stage of working toward your goal. Discuss the areas in which you think you need advice. At this point, ask your set of prepared questions.

Step 12: Ask for Suggestions

It is also extremely important that you remember the information your potential mentor, and later on your mentor, provides. You accomplish this by taking copious notes. You want to write down every single thing your mentor says regarding your questions. Afterwards, you might ask for specific suggestions regarding problems you might have. If he offers advice, consider yourself lucky.

Step 13: Trial Close

Next comes the "trial close." It is just like the trial close in a sales transaction, only here you are selling yourself. You are also selling this person on the idea of becoming your mentor. The trial close is a way of asking him to make a commitment. The reason it is called a *trial* close is because you are not asking him point-blank to be your mentor. You need him to warm up to the idea, so you float a kind of trial offer. One of the best ways to do that is to ask, "Who were your mentors? Who were the people that had a strong effect on you?" Then you say, "Are you mentoring anybody now?" If he says yes, ask who they are and why they chose him. Then say, "The reason I'm asking is that the ideas you have shared with me have really sparked my imagination as well as my enthusiasm and my passion to succeed. It would be great if someday I could earn the right to be your protégé and be mentored by you. I wonder what it would take for me to earn an opportunity to have you as my mentor?"

When you word it this way, you are raising his status. The key is to ask what you can do to "earn an opportunity" to be mentored by him. When you put it this way, it dignifies him and enhances his achievements. He will be much more inclined to grant you what you are asking for. Choosing the right words during the trial close is extremely important in getting your potential mentor to say yes. (It sometimes helps to practice this with a friend in a role-playing session before the meeting.)

Step 14: Send Thank-You Note, Gift

At this point, you are not actually asking the person to be your mentor, you are just *suggesting* it. That is as far as you want to go for now. You want to thank him for his time, insight, and wisdom. After the meeting, you want to send a follow-up note thanking him again. If appropriate, send him a token gift. It could be anything, usually small. If you are just getting started, you aren't going to be able to afford a large or extravagant gift. The gift you send should be thoughtful, however.

Let's say your potential mentor is female, and she enjoys playing tennis. You discover she loves Disneyland. She and her family go there all the time. They have season passes, in fact. She thinks Mickey Mouse is cute, and she collects figurines. You might call Disneyland and find out if they have any Mickey Mouse tennis balls. You send her a tube of these as a token thank-you.

Your gift should show her that you really listened, that you have an imagination, and that you are willing to go an extra creative mile to say thank you. You are establishing that you go above and beyond the ordinary. It's another selling point supporting why she should consider being your mentor.

Say you find out your prospective male mentor is wild about bass fishing. You shop around and finally locate a store that carries bass fishing paraphernalia. Maybe there is a brand-new lure that he has never tried before, so you send it to him

It takes initiative and creativity to send a token gift that's appropriate. Make a mental note that as your relationship continues to grow, you will be sure to acknowledge the value of your mentor.

One of our colleagues, author Jeff Davidson, initiated an annual award several years ago to formally recognize mentors who had helped his career. Jeff is highly enthusiastic about the mentoring process. Here is a reprint of the actual letter Jeff sent to one of his award-winning mentors.

> Good morning [recipient's name]:
>
> At this time each year, I reflect on the year that recently passed and determine who had the greatest impact on my career, work, and life. You are the 199- recipient of the "Jeff Davidson Mentor Award."
>
> I base this award *not* on how much time people happened to have spent with me, although that can be an important factor, but what I learned or gained from them. Your timely advice has enabled me to accelerate my career (launched as a full-time venture only in January 199-).
>
> I carefully considered everything you told me and followed nearly all of it.

Thank you [first name] for your continuing contributions.

Sincerely,

Jeff Davidson

Here is the list of the Jeff Davidson Mentor Award recipients that he has kept faithfully for years.

1981   Deenie Kenner—A friend with far-eastern wisdom, a gentle manner, and eternal patience.

1982   Jon Pearson—A co-worker and friend to all, who leads by example everyday of his life.

1983   Richard A. Connor—A mentor and friend who showed me the power and potential that the entrepreneurial life could provide.

1984   Betty Arbuckle—My first and only life coach, who opened up the door to seeing things in other ways.

1985   Dr. Harvey Austin—A new friend who, in the span of 30 minutes, convinced me that my quest for self-improvement could take a megaleap.

1986   Bonita Nelson—The only literary agent who took the trouble to sell my second and third books, which helped launch my career as an author.

1987   Pat McGallum—A consummate seminar leader and high spirit on earth who shows how to make profound and effective choices in all aspects of my life.

1988   Holland Cooke—My personal guide in the world of broadcasting.

1989   Dave Yoho—A co-author who has a profound sense of business and ethics and knows what works in life.

1990   Ron Wagner—A godsend in the form of a personal PC guru who opened up a world on possibilities for me in my own home office.

1991   Ron Wagner—Further extending my career outlook and capabilities through timely advice, upgrades, on-the-spot training, and high accessibility.

1992   Dottie Walters—The queen of sharing ideas among speakers who personally and profoundly helped me accelerate my speaking career.

1993   Elizabeth Jeffries—A professional's professional in the speaking business whose insights are profound and eternal.

1994   Tony Alessandra—A master of the spoken and written word whose business acumen is uncanny and in great demand.

1995   Rob Sommer—A video producer with an eye towards bringing out the best in a speaker.

As you can tell, Jeff has considerable experience as a protégé and undoubtedly has learned a tremendous amount from his mentors. He understands the benefits of the mentoring process. But one of the most important things he never fails to do for his mentors is to properly thank them for their time and energy helping him.

Steps 15 and 16: Evaluate Information, Take Action

After your first meeting with your prospective mentor you will want to do some evaluation. Go home and review the information in your notes. As you are looking it over, there are going to be things that you like and things you don't care for. If you generally like the advice he or she has given, you have to start moving on the tasks your prospective mentor has suggested, even though you might be a little hesitant, or you think you are taking a chance on this person.

When you start taking the advice and following up on the suggestions of your potential mentor, some things are going to go very smoothly, and you will think, "Why didn't I think of that?" Other areas won't go as well, and you very likely are going to run into obstacles. People you approach with your ideas may slam the door in your face. It is going to be hard, and you are going to take a few lumps. You may think the advice you got was bad because nothing is working.

Step 17: Call Mentor with Results

The key is to try to accomplish your tasks and get past this hurdle, regardless of how much opposition you run into. You almost always will be in a better position than when you started. Once you have a few results from your efforts, report back to your mentor. Just call the mentor on the phone and say, "Hello, Mr. Jones. This is _____. I just wanted to follow up with you and thank you for the advice you shared with me. I'm moving ahead with the steps you suggested, and several are really working great. I'm just really pleased—I can't thank you enough. You told me to do X, Y and Z, and I did X, Y, and Z, and it all worked really well."

Then you say, "In addition to that, I have tried steps A, B, and C. With A, B, and C, I had a little bit more difficulty." You then describe the obstacles where you felt challenged. "I was wondering if you could offer some additional advice on how I could handle these," you continue.

Once you tell him about the successes you had, praise him for the information he gave you and show him you took action on his tasks (even though you still have challenges). He will be willing to provide additional advice to accomplish your goal. Then you say, "Yes, that's a great idea; thank you very much. I'm going to do exactly what you are saying. If I may, I would like to call you back in about three weeks and let you know what happened as a result of this step. Will that be all right with you?"

He will say, "Absolutely—let me know what happens." We never have had anyone respond, "I don't want to hear about what happens to you from now on!" The reason is that mentors are now vested; they have spent time with you, and you are proving their advice to be valuable. Some of the things they told you to do are working. And they will want to know what happens with their ideas. It's important for a teacher to know that his or her student is learning. Eventually, the mentor will not only be vested, but will genuinely *care*.

Steps 18 and 19: Set the Second Appointment

At this point you will want to evaluate the responses your prospective mentor gives you on the telephone. If you like what he says, and it feels good, follow his advice once again and put his ideas to the test. Three weeks later when you call, ask to meet again. The conversation may go something like this: "You know what? I just don't know how to thank you for all of the information that you have given me. It's been invaluable. I would really like the opportunity to take you to lunch and thank you again, if you wouldn't mind. Besides, I have several very interesting things that have happened since we talked that I am dying to share with you."

The appointment could be for lunch, or even breakfast, or maybe you will stop by his or her office again. Perhaps you can say, "I've come across a couple of articles I think you would be interested in, and I would like to show them to you at the meeting." You are thus expressing an interest in and willingness to do something for them.

You can't possibly repay him the dollar value of the information he has given you, but you can let him know you appreciate his time. One way to do so is through contributing your time to a philanthropic effort in which he is interested. While asking for your second appointment, say, "You know, I don't know how to thank you for all of the advice you have given me, but I do know that you are very involved in the March of Dimes (American Cancer Society, Children's Miracle Network, etc.)—is there anything I can do for you in terms of your association work that would perhaps serve as a thank you for all the time you have invested in me?"

Steps 20 and 21: Propose the Mentoring Relationship

You go to your second appointment. If things seem to be clicking, this is a good time to ask about a mentoring relationship. Following your earlier trial close, you now employ what we call in sales "the actual close." He may ask you what is involved because he might not have mentored anyone before. If he has questions, say that you came across this book which lists guidelines for mentoring that seem to make a lot of sense. Just say, "I thought I would share them with you, and if these make sense to you too, then we both can follow them." Then take him through the 16 Laws of Mentoring (see next chapter) in order to set a positive tone and mutually agreeable standards for the relationship.

Once you have completed this process—all 21 steps—you will be able to do it again with someone else. You also will repeat the process many times, with a few variations, when selecting your secondary mentors.

While learning these 21 steps may seem a bit daunting at first, you must remember that you are undertaking to persuade someone to invest his or her most precious asset—him- or herself—in your future. You have a selling job to do convincing mentors that you are truly worth what will amount to a substantial investment. This process takes a little finesse, but if you practice, you will find that you are suddenly able to persuade someone you admire to become your mentor. Eventually you will want to pick and choose your mentors strategically, and you will want to find knowledgeable specialists who have current information not available from books.

The following is the story of how Mary Rudisill, a consultant in Keizer, Oregan, found her mentor—she simply asked.

"POPPING THE QUESTION"

Feeling overwhelmed, I sat in my room trying to figure out where to start. There was so much to learn in the speaking business. The heaviness of fatigue made it hard to think clearly, so I said a short prayer asking for direction and lay down to take a nap. Upon awakening I had an interesting thought: Call Carol Peterson, a professional speaker whose work I respect, and ask her, if you were her daughter and wanted to learn the business, how would she help you?

I lay there debating whether I should call. A flood of doubts and fears filled my mind. Would she think I was too pushy? Would she laugh and think that was a ridiculous idea? Would she feel obligated and afraid to say no? Would she want to help me?

Finally I asked myself, what is the worst thing that she could say? The answer was "No." So I decided to call. I had nothing to lose if she said no, and if she said yes, a lot to gain. As the phone rang I rehearsed how I would ask the question, but when she answered I said: "Hi, Carol, this is Mary Rudisill from National Speakers Association. I called to ask you something. Well, ahh, I would like to know. . . you are under no obligation . . . I was thinking that if . . . ahh OK, I'll just come right out and ask. I was thinking, if I were your daughter and needed help getting started in the speaking business, as my mother, would you be willing to help me?"

Then I sat there in dead silence, grimacing, waiting for her response. To my surprise and delight she said, "Mary, I would be honored."

I couldn't believe my ears. She said she felt "honored" that I asked her!

continues

concluded

And what an honor it has been for me, too. We have spent the last year meeting and sharing by phone. I have grown so much in one short year, it's sometimes hard to believe. And to my surprise in April I received the "President's Rookie of the Year Award," from our Oregon Speakers Association, a chapter of the National Speakers Association.

This award recognized me for my developmental achievements. I know that having a mentor like Carol has helped me by a quantum leap. Why Carol Peterson? From the first day I met her she struck me as the personification of a professional, with integrity and class. I admired how she presented herself, the image she projected, and that she was genuinely nice. When I first met her she treated me with such respect, she listened and spoke to me like I was someone of importance.

If any one wonders whether a mentor would be important to them professionally, let there be no doubt, the answer is "yes."

Carol and I have not only grown professionally, but also as friends. She said that being a mentor has helped her grow in new directions. A mentor has given me the mirroring I needed to develop as well as the inner strength that came from a "mother/daughter" connection, which enriched both our lives.

So as you search for your "kindred spirit," remember, you become as your teacher, therefore select with care.

REFLECTIONS ON THE MENTOR/PROTÉGÉ RELATIONSHIP

The satisfaction that protégés receive from having a good mentor is hard to describe. There is a sense of gratitude that is truly humbling, particularly in a young person. Here is a letter that was sent to Alice O'Connor, a communications consultant in Madison, Wisconsin, that will give you a feeling for the profound effect a mentor can have on a person.

Dear Alice,

It has been an absolute pleasure working for you. I have learned many things over the past year, and the fact that I am going to have a job (although I haven't decided where) is due to the fact that I had this internship experience. People say it over and over again, "Wow, I am so impressed you've done all of this work. Most graduates come in to an interview with their academic writing." I just smile and think of all the times you said, "Work on this, it will be great for your portfolio." I went from knowing nothing about politics to being able to have an intelligent conversation with someone about the subject. I learned how to write memos and how to separate the important stuff from the rest in a hearing or interview. I've seen what it's like to be a professional woman in a man's world. The things I've learned professionally are innumerable, and I thank you for that.

However, I have learned something more important than any lesson I could have taken away with me professionally, and that is that I have learned what kind of person I want to be, concluded in large part from working for you. I don't think I ever left work not feeling good about myself. I have always been so hard on myself if everything doesn't go perfectly and as a result, my image of myself was skewed. However, I had a role model to look up to and that was you.

I've seen you make mistakes and have bad days, but you keep on going. You don't give up. You work later at night to get stuff done for work yet still make time for your family. You give speeches to professional organizations but still take the time to talk to high school kids about how to be successful. The broad range of your work has influenced so many people, and I hope that you realize that. And you have a sense of humor and a life—I love it. My quote for this internship and to sum everything up is from Newton: "If I see farther, it's because I stand on the great shoulders of giants."

Wherever I go in my career, I was so lucky to learn some of the ropes from one of the best. I appreciate all the time and effort I know you spent to make this a valuable experience for me, and I assure you, you succeeded. I have to admit some people have not and will not get as much out of this internship as I did. However, if they get even a fraction, it is definitely worth their while.

That is a powerful testimonial from a protégé who spent time with a good mentor—someone who was willing to trust a young person enough to give them sufficient responsibility to build up their self-confidence with positive experiences, someone who provided a positive role model for them to think about as they struggled to establish themselves in a career.

The fact is, mentoring can have a very positive effect on your career and can establish you on the fast track to success. In a 1993 article titled "The Relationship of Career Mentoring to Early Career Outcomes," published in the journal *Organizational Studies*, researchers found that Belgian business graduates were far more likely to find satisfaction in their work as well as their careers if they had been mentored early in their professional lives. The researchers also found that those who were mentored received significantly more promotions than those who weren't!

In this chapter we have shown you a few of the many benefits of becoming a protégé and listed the major qualifications that you must possess in order for your mentoring experience to be a success. We also have given you a list of places to begin looking for your mentor. Learning the details of the 21 steps to choosing your mentor may take several readings, but the process is simple enough, really. And it does work. Armed with these tools, you will be able to approach nearly anyone whom you wish to request to become your mentor.

In the next chapter, we will cover the laws that we developed to guide both the mentor and protégé into a lasting mentor/protégé relationship. These laws will help ensure that your mentoring experience is a success.

HIGHLIGHTS

❖ Protégés are expected to earn the right to mentor-provided opportunities and should not expect payment in exchange for a chance to realize their own dreams.

❖ A mentor may open career doors for a protégé, save the protégé time and money, and also benefit the protégé in many intangible ways.

❖ Among the qualifications of being a good protégé are a willingness to respect the mentor's time and the determination to follow through on his or her advice.

❖ Finding a mentor may be challenging, but a good place to start is your local library.

❖ From setting your goal to making a mutual commitment with your mentor, the 21 steps to choosing your mentor is a complete set of instructions for entering into the mentoring process.

❖ Research shows mentoring results in more career satisfaction and promotions.

CHAPTER

On Becoming a Mentor

A true mentor does two things: believes in a person and has absolutely no feelings of competition. Sue Pivetta

Becoming a Mentor—What's in It for Me?

Having diligently read through the first four chapters of this book, you know about the many types and variations of mentoring, and you have solid evidence that it has led to career success and personal satisfaction for many people, some of them famous. However, for those who are reading this during precious time between meetings, around deadlines, amidst major projects, after jet-lag, and in between picking up the kids at school, adopting a mentoring lifestyle might sound like something to postpone until your life slows down a little. Perhaps you will consider being someone's mentor when you are old and wise enough to pass along all your hard-earned knowledge to some youthful protégé and can do so at a respectable pace and with the grace of a master statesman.

It is the very fact that you see yourself as overextended, overworked, underpaid, and unappreciated, with little or no time to spare that creates the best argument of all for why you should now consider becoming someone's mentor.

We are reminded of a story we heard in church one Sunday about a family of East European refugees, driven from their home by invading soldiers, who decide their only chance of escaping the horrors of war is to make it through the mountains that surround their village. They are sure they will find safety in a neighboring neutral country, if only they can make it over the pass. The grandfather is not well, however, and the days of his mountain hiking are long past.

"Leave me behind," he pleads. "The soldiers won't bother with an old man like me."

"Yes, they will," warns the son. "It will mean your grave."

"We can't leave you behind, Grandpa," implores the daughter. "If you won't go, then we won't either."

The old man finally relents, and the family, which numbers some 10 people of varying ages, including the daughter's year-old baby girl, sets off after dark toward the blue-black mountain range in the distance. As they walk along silently, each takes a turn carrying the baby, whose weight makes travel more difficult, as they wind their way up the steep mountain pass. After several hours, the grandfather sits down on a rock and hangs his head. "Go on without me," he says in a low voice. "I can't make it."

"Yes you can," his son implores. "You have to."

"No," says the old man. "Leave me here."

"Come on," says the son. "We need you—it's your turn to carry the baby."

The old man looks up and sees the tired faces of the others in the group. He looks at the baby wrapped in a blanket and being carried now in the arms of his thin, 13-year-old grandson.

"Yes, of course," says the old man. "It's my turn. Come, give her to me." He stands up and takes the baby in his arms and looks into her small, innocent face. Suddenly he feels a renewed strength and a powerful desire to see his family find safety in a land where war is a distant memory.

"Come on," he says with a note of determination in his voice. "Let's go. I'm fine now. I just needed to rest. Let's keep moving." They all headed up the hill again with the grandfather carrying the baby.

The family reached safety that night, and everyone who started the long journey through the mountains finished it—including the old man.

The point is that having the responsibility for looking after someone else gives us the will and energy to reach new heights we never dreamed were attainable—*until we had to do it*. Becoming a mentor will not only benefit your protégé—it will benefit you!

Say you feel pressured, but you are at the top of your field and your time and services are in constant demand. Your knowledge and skills are perfected, and you are at the pinnacle of your career. It is now that you are best equipped to teach some talented person—who may or may not be younger than you are—what you have learned over the years. You have the power to help others. We will now discuss the various benefits that come from mentoring, the qualifications you need to be a mentor, and finally, how to select a protégé. You will see the advantages of being both a mentor and a protégé, that it is better to give than to receive, that life comes around full circle, and those who give are those who get.

THE SIX BENEFITS OF MENTORING

We believe that to adopt the mentoring lifestyle means that you become both a mentor and a protégé, regardless of your level of accomplishment. It is not only the skills and knowledge that you can acquire through this lifestyle that are important; the spiritual renewal and sense of self-worth are equally, if not more, important. Through our research on mentoring and the many studies that have been conducted to determine its effect on individuals, we have identified six leading reasons why you should consider becoming a mentor. We believe the sixth is at the heart of what it means to adopt the mentoring lifestyle. Mentoring accomplishes the following:

1. Carries on your legacy.
2. Keeps you sharp.
3. Forces you to set an example, thereby enhancing performance.
4. Enhances your value to others.
5. Encourages creativity.
6. Provides a window to "get by giving."

Some people have incorporated a formal mentoring program into their business operations and structured it so that both they and their protégés accomplish more than either could achieve alone. Insurance agent Betsy Cash Woolfolk, CLU, ChFC, of Richmond, Virginia, is a member of the Minnesota Mutual Life Insurance Company's Chairman's Club, the company's leading female producer, and was honored by the Richmond Association of Life Underwriters as agent of the year. Here is her story, taken with her permission from an article that appeared in the December 1992 issue of *Life Insurance Selling* magazine:

HOW PROTEGES BOOSTED MY CAREER, INCOME, AND LIFE

After eight years in the life insurance business, I reached a plateau in the family market. By any objective standard, I was doing well enough, but I no longer was challenged. I had achieved Million Dollar Round Table (MDRT) production several years earlier and found it difficult to visualize how I could continue to grow. Much of my work took place in the evening, and because I could see no more than two appointments each night, it appeared I had reached a production ceiling. I was growing bored and frustrated. I needed to find a way to expand into more advanced markets. But how? My comfort zone in the family market was well established, and the path to other markets eluded me. That was in 1987. Since then, I not only have found success in the advanced markets—I have rediscovered the challenge and opportunity for service and income that originally attracted me to life insurance.

Today, instead of selling around the kitchen table with the kids looking on, I am in the boardroom with corporate decision makers and their advisers. The cases I have developed in this market have enabled me to break through my plateau and quadruple my production, and unlike my years in the family market, virtually all of my sales activity now takes place during regular business hours. My experience has proven to me that the business market is more accessible than most agents believe, but the first step was not easy. My biggest hurdle at the beginning was making a commitment to prospect among business owners in spite of how little I knew about how to work in this market.

I knew with the right telephone track I could get appointments, but what would I say after I got there? I lacked technical knowledge and was intimidated, even frightened, by the likelihood of embarrassing myself in front of a substantial prospect.

continues

continued

I realize now that if had I waited to call on business owners until I was comfortable with my knowledge of business insurance, I would still be waiting. My growth in the business market was accelerated when my general agent implemented a structured mentoring program designed to jump-start new agents in their careers and increase the productivity of senior agents. Based on the mentor program developed by Richard McCloskey in his Irvine, California, agency, our program enables me and other established producers to act as mentors for several classes of new agents each year.

Each new protégé agent I mentor is responsible for prospecting in advanced markets and must provide me a certain number of appointments each week. I am responsible for developing and closing as many of these cases as possible, as quickly as possible, which enables the young agent to learn through repetitive observation.

Initially, I was nervous about being a mentor because I would have to assume some financial responsibility for the new hire. I was a novice in the business market at the time and hardly considered myself successful enough to assume such a role. But I agreed to become a mentor when I recognized the enormous prospecting benefits would more than compensate me for my efforts, and my general agent promised the volume of activity the program would create would enable me to sharpen my skills and accelerate my growth in advanced sales. He was right!

My activity has more than doubled as a result of the mentor program. For several years now, I have averaged 15 to 20 appointments a week, with 6 to 8 being new prospects. At this activity level, I can focus on the most desirable prospects, delegate the others, and take more risks in the sales process. About 70 percent of my premiums in 1991, more than $200,000, were a direct result of appointments obtained for me through the mentor program. But the activity this program creates has done much more than enable me to increase my production substantially. It kept me focused and busy seeing people during a time in my life when personal tragedy threatened to overwhelm me.

In January 1991, I was diagnosed with breast cancer. I underwent surgery, followed by seven and a half months of chemotherapy. My grief and fear for the future were overwhelming and might have consumed me, resulting in my not producing for months. Instead, because of the continuous flow of appointments scheduled for me by the new agents in the mentor program, I was too busy to allow my illness to get the better of me.

continues

concluded

While sensitive to my limitations, the young agents to whom I was committed as mentor nonetheless needed me to meet with the advanced prospects they continued to schedule. Because I was needed and felt responsible for helping these agents make sales, I somehow kept myself going. More than once I went straight from chemotherapy into the field. I credit the sense of mission created for me by the mentor program with enabling me not only to survive a potentially devastating year, but to emerge from it stronger and with greater optimism than before.

Today, I am totally immersed in business insurance, and I believe there is nothing about my transition to this market that cannot be duplicated by other agents. For those other agents who want to enter this lucrative market, I have three guidelines that have been fundamental to my career growth:

1. Don't be afraid to step out of your comfort zone and stay out of it. The fastest way to grow professionally is to take some risk and learn as you go. Eleanor Roosevelt said that the only way to conquer fear is to do what you fear and keep doing it until you develop a series of successful experiences. Initially the agent may be technically weak, as I was, but he or she almost always will know more than his or her prospects.
2. Commit to high appointment activity. Without many opportunities every week to develop knowledge and skills, it will be years, if ever, before the agent becomes adept and established in this market. The agent cannot learn as he goes if he's not going.
3. Associate with an agency committed to helping the agent realize his full potential. Ultimately, each of us must take responsibility for creating our own success, but none of us can do it alone. I owe much of my growth to the frequent encouragement and continuous assistance I receive from my general agent and my agency colleagues. Don't underestimate the impact the right agency can have on the agent's career or the benefits of becoming a mentor.

Five years ago, as I faced a plateau in the family market, advanced sales seemed out of reach—something only older, smarter, or better-connected agents got into. I since have discovered the business market not only is more accessible than I thought, but also more fun and rewarding than I believed possible. And mentoring helped me to achieve more than I ever imagined.

As you can see, mentoring helped Betsy Cash Woolfolk in many ways. She was able to break into a supposedly "unreachable" market and grow in ways she never anticipated. Furthermore, the expectations placed upon her by her protégés kept her going through the ordeal of fighting cancer.

The benefits Betsy cites are only a few that come from the successful practice of mentoring. Let's take a look at each of the six major benefits in greater detail.

Mentoring Carries on Your Legacy

The first benefit of having a protégé is that your protégé can carry on your legacy. When you have created something or come up with something innovative, you naturally want that work to carry on after you are gone. Hopefully you will instill that information and knowledge in a protégé, and he or she will carry on what you have started. This is important from a number of perspectives. There is an adage that states that those who do not learn from history are doomed to repeat it. The truth in this statement as regards mentoring lies within the fact that you can save somebody time, money, sanity, and security and at the same time display your accomplishments to the world. It gives you a way to extend your life experience. We have an implied responsibility to future generations to impart knowledge to those who come after us.

Mentoring Keeps You Sharp

The best possible way to learn something is to teach it to someone else. Dealing with a protégé in search of information is a great way for the mentor to stay mentally sharp. Many times, we will initiate a brainstorming session that touches on numerous areas of business. Floyd will counsel Terri, and, as often as not, inspire an approach or generate an idea that he realizes he should be implementing at his own company. Floyd says, "I begin telling Terri to do something, then I realize I'm not even doing it myself. It could be an area that I need to return to in order to improve my own presentation. Mentoring Terri works really well to keep me sharp."

Helping someone less experienced keeps you up to date on the things that you may need to pass down to your team that you haven't reinforced in a while. Furthermore, being up on the topics your protégé will ask about helps you create and maintain a valid checklist of action items. As you teach somebody else, you automatically develop your own mental checklist of things you need to accomplish. Instruction is a great way to use *self-talk*, the concept pioneered by Dr. Shad Helmstetter, in which you state, using the first-person present tense, the action you want to be taking, and the rest of you eventually just starts following along! Often, the problems that your protégé is going through are very similar to problems that you may be going through on your own but in a different way. As you are walking through the process on the protégé's end, you are talking yourself through it, which is extremely valuable in solving problems. You come out of the experience feeling empowered.

You Set an Example for Others

Serving as a mentor forces you to set an example for others—and this creates a better you. It is odd, but when you are teaching somebody else, you cross all your *t*s and dot all your *i*s. You know somebody is watching, and that forces you to do your best. You are setting the example for someone who expects you to show him how to do things correctly. You can't let him down; you have to practice what you preach, and this spurs you to try harder. It is a great way to stay motivated, because the inspiration comes from within.

Your Value to Others Increases

You will increase your value to others if you share your wisdom and a desirable vision. In this constantly changing world, the ability to teach others is an asset. It's not uncommon for management to express a position such as, "We need to keep that person on board," or "We need to promote this person to a higher level because they have the ability to train and inspire others." The old cliché, "those who can—do; those who can't—teach," is ridiculous. It is often more difficult to teach someone to do something well than it is to do it yourself. Terri reports she is frequently challenged by protégés who need her to explain things in detail:

> A classic illustration for me has been writing this book. I know exactly what I need to do in order to get involved in a mentoring rela-

tionship, but when I sit down with a young person who has come to me asking, "Well, what do I do?," it's difficult to know what to tell them. When you know how to do something naturally, you just do it. There is no explanation. When you have somebody say, "But, I don't understand. What do I do next?" you have to lay it out play-by-play and walk them through each step of the process. It can be very tedious and difficult.

Floyd notes that if you are successful at training and inspiring others, it is not uncommon for people to perceive you as knowledgeable and talented. They are impressed when they see you can train others.

Your Personal Creativity Is Enhanced

Mentoring helps you exercise your personal creativity. Meeting with your protégé forces you to provide a variety of options, or action steps, that the person can take. When you are supplying all of these options you are challenging yourself to come up with the answers. You are thinking creatively, putting things together that you might otherwise not have had the incentive to associate. You are coming up with actionable ideas that you can take back to your own business or family. To get creative, you have to step out of the box. Don't look just at what you see within the box but at all the possibilities. A protégé can help you just by sharing his or thoughts. Reflect on your protégé's thought processes, and use your own knowledge to determine where it is lacking. It's always easier to critique somebody else than to critique yourself. It shows you a mirror image of your ideas without the discomfort of someone else critiquing you.

You Get by Giving

There are untold riches to be acquired by living according to the adage "You get by giving." Before Terri started her own company, she had been a promoter of other sales trainers and speakers for three years. A young woman named Darlene Lyons, who had just started a company called Peak Performance Enterprises, called her on the phone and asked, 'Terri, I'd really like to learn how you promoted these big events. I'm starting my own company. What should I do?'

Terri told her she would be happy to meet with her. "She said that she would gladly pay me for my time, so I said, 'Fine, it will be $150 an hour.' When we got to lunch, I could see that she and her associate were really struggling. They needed a lot of help, and I ended up spending about two and a half hours with them. I empathized with their situation and I actually learned a lot from just trying to teach them the basics. I ended up picking up the lunch tab and not charging them anything. But I had gained a new contact. Five years later, when her company had grown into an organization that promoted very large events, Darlene called me and asked me to speak. This engagement led to eight other well-paid bookings in the same year plus the invaluable exposure and new contacts I made. All of this came from a lunch that paid for itself a hundred times over."

FIREMAN'S FIELD DAY

There was a time," says Floyd, "when I was flat broke and had a bad self-image and bad habits. I started studying success principles, and one of them had to do with the word, "love." Love, of course, means a lot of things, but for certain, love is giving—not taking. So I started practicing this when I was in my late 20s, and I have tried to be giving of my time and knowledge ever since. The impact of what this approach to life can do for you was brought home years ago in a dramatic way. One day after work I was sitting in a restaurant having a drink when a Detroit fireman walks in selling Field Day tickets for $1 apiece. He walks up to me and asks, "Can I sell you a Field Day ticket?"

"Sure," I say. "Here's a buck." So he gives me the ticket and starts walking away. I thought for a second and called him back. "Excuse me," I said, "But if you don't mind, let me give you a little technique that might help you." (You can tell that by now I had become the type of person who wants to help everybody!) I told him to ask his first question, but then follow it up when the prospect says yes with another question—"How many kids do you have?" I told him, whatever that number is, peel off that many tickets. "Hey, that's a great technique," he says. "By the way, how many kids do *you* have?" I said I had three, and he handed me two more tickets. I smiled and

continues

> concluded
>
> handed him two more dollars. Six weeks later, I got a call informing me that my raffle ticket was picked at random at the Fireman's Field Day and that I had just won a Lincoln Continental Mark IV. Which ticket do you suppose won the prize? The third one, of course!

You may not win a car as a result of becoming a mentor, but you may win the hearts of people who will be forever grateful for your gift. But mentoring is not for everyone. It takes time, and there are risks. In order to determine whether or not you are ready to become a mentor, here is a list of qualifications we believe are necessary.

QUALIFICATIONS FOR BECOMING A MENTOR

1. Give time unselfishly.
2. Possess a desired skill or experience.
3. Be willing to share your knowledge.
4. Make a commitment.

Give Time Unselfishly

The foremost requirement for being a mentor is that you must be willing to give unselfishly of your time. You can't always be asking yourself, "What's in it for me?" You have to be able to say, "I'm just going to help this person out because I could have used a little help way back when." If the gift of your time comes back to you, great. If it doesn't, that's fine too. We believe strongly in the get-by-giving philosophy, but if you are going into mentoring looking for something in return, we don't think you are going to get it. It has to be unselfish.

Possess Valuable Experience

You have to have experience that a protégé would find valuable. You can't just take on a protégé and expect that they are going to be your servant. That is not a protégé's job. As a mentor, you need to be able to empower protégés. In the process, you will be empowered.

Willingly Share Knowledge

You should have a desire to share your experience with and help other people. Once you realize you have valuable experience that might be worthwhile to somebody else, you need to take the next step. You could be the world's most intelligent person, with an encyclopedic knowledge of one or a number of subjects, but if you can't communicate that information, it is worth little. You have to be able to get information into the mind of somebody else in order for it to have value. It is the same with mentoring; you might have a wealth of experience that a protégé would find valuable, but you also need to have the desire to share that experience.

Make a Commitment

Finally, you must make a definite commitment. You can't just snap your fingers and expect mentoring to work for you. Sometimes you are going to meet people who are just one-hit wonders, as they say in the music industry. You have one meeting with them and you never hear from them again. At other times, you will meet people who are going to want to draw on your experience over a longer period. You just have to chalk it up as part of the overall experience and keep at it. The following story from one of our protégés who became a mentor shows how making a commitment to a protégé can create stress even though it is ultimately worth it.

> Recently, I was having a really hectic workday. I had six projects on my desk and very much wanted to get them all done before I left for vacation. Phones were ringing off the hook because it was summer, and everybody else was about go on vacation as well. I get a call from a young man who I am mentoring by telephone. I think to myself, "This is not the right day to be talking to him. I don't have time right now to take a half-hour out to mentor someone." Nevertheless, I took a deep breath and said, "OK, I made a commitment to this and said I would help. I also said if he called me on Friday, I would take the phone call."
>
> "OK," I said, "How much time do you need?"
> "I need about 15 minutes," he said.

"OK, the clock's on."

It ended up that by talking him through the process with which he needed help, I ended up much more relaxed and was able to accomplish my tasks even more effectively. He just made me stop, look, and then refocus. My commitment paid off with improvements to my sanity at the workplace.

Mentoring is not a ride on easy street. If you sincerely care, you can easily spend twice the time figuring out how to teach as your protégé does in learning. You must be committed enough to willingly share your time and knowledge, and make a concerted effort to mentor in a field you know something about.

HOW TO FIND, SELECT, AND BEGIN WORKING WITH A PROTÉGÉ

There are eight steps to choosing the right protégé. While we believe that everyone should have a protégé, we don't believe that you should pick *just any* protégé. The eight steps listed here are intended to allow you to identify candidates and screen them according to your personal preferences. As a mentor, your time is valuable, and it is important that you select a protégé who is committed and will respect both your time and knowledge.

1. Determine your strengths and weaknesses.
2. Identify the characteristics of your ideal protégé.
3. Spread the word to colleagues.
4. Prequalify protégé candidates.
5. Select interview candidates.
6. Invite them to tell you their life story.
7. Select the protégé.
8. Commit together to the 16 Laws of Mentoring.

First, you must do a self-analysis and determine your strengths and weaknesses as a potential mentor. Do you have special knowledge or skills? Do you have any hobbies of which you are particularly proud? What would you have fun talking about with someone less experienced than yourself? Given these factors, you must decide on the ideal characteristics of your protégé. The traits to look for depend on your industry, what you hope to impart, the person's enthusiasm level, and so on.

Next you have to start spreading the word. Networking in search of a protégé is similar to looking for a job or a new employee. Begin with your colleagues and let them know that you are interested in working with someone. For instance, perhaps you want to work with someone who is two years out of college—someone who is a little hungry and who has drive and long-term goals to work in your industry—someone who is willing to make the investment.

Once you throw your line out, people start to gravitate toward you. You may not have a large choice. Maybe you get only one or two candidates. In any case, this is when you start to prequalify them. First you want to check and make sure they are truly interested and committed. You have to go through a screening process that will help you determine the candidate you want to spend time with.

We suggest that you first have them write you a letter that answers a few questions. After all, if they are really interested in your sharing your time with them at no cost, they are going to have to share their thoughts on a couple of subjects. These include:

- ❖ Why did they select this particular field of endeavor?
- ❖ Why are they so passionate about this?
- ❖ What made them choose to do it?
- ❖ What are their accomplishments to date in reaching their goal?
- ❖ What is their level of commitment? On a scale of 1 to 10, are they committed at level 5, 6, or at the very top? Are they 110 percent committed?
- ❖ What are their feelings about taking direction from a mentor? Ask them to relate a story where someone gave them advice, they acted on it, and it worked.
- ❖ Do they thoroughly understand the process?
- ❖ Tell them that if you agree to work with them, you do not intend to waste time. Then ask them flat out why they are worthy of being mentored by you!

Select candidates for interviews from the letters you get back. Set up meetings to last from a half-hour to an hour. Ask the candidates to tell their life stories. These will give you even greater insight into who they are and what their goals are. Select the person you think would be the best protégé *for you*. You might even select two at the same time because one could drop out. Have them read, understand, and commit to the 16 Laws of Mentoring. You are looking for a protégé who eventually will become another mentor, and you will want to instill in that person the process of the mentoring relationship. Later on, he or she will end up doing the same thing for someone else. You are creating a self-perpetuating process intended to improve society as a whole.

Personality Traits of a Successful Protégé

When looking for a protégé you will want to find a suitable personality type. According to an article published in the June 1994 *Academy of Management Journal,* researchers found a correlation between certain personality traits and successful protégés. "Successful" here means only that they *had become* protégés and had positioned themselves in such a way as to have mentors commit to helping them. Of course the researchers also found that these same people were more successful in their careers *because* they were protégés.

The researchers, Dr. Thomas Dougherty, then professor of management, and Dr. Daniel B. Turban, assistant professor of management at the University of Missouri, correlated three personality traits with a person's likelihood of becoming a mentor. They found that a person was more apt to initiate a protégé relationship with a mentor the more he believed he could personally influence his own success. Other positive indicators were the person's sensitivity to other people's behavior (social cues) and how high was his overall level of self esteem.

Author Pam Grout, in her booklet *The Mentoring Advantage: How to Help Your Career Soar to New Heights* (SkillPath Publications, Mission, KS, 1995) offers a list of nearly a dozen characteristics that she believes go along with being a promising protégé candidate. They include:

- ❖ Has clearly defined goals
- ❖ Is willing to take direction
- ❖ Can accept help
- ❖ Listens to what others say

❖ Can follow detailed instructions

❖ Expresses gratitude

❖ Can be assertive when the occasion calls for it

❖ Isn't afraid to ask for help if he needs it

❖ Has self-confidence

❖ Follows through on assignments

❖ Is a team player and shares the credit for a job well done

REFLECTIONS ON MENTORING

Sam Cupp is a successful Michigan businessman who has worked to establish mentoring programs for young people throughout his region. He believes in a disciplined approach to mentoring, one that emphasizes detailed life planning:

> Having mentors has meant all the difference in the world to me and to my career. Mentoring is several steps beyond advice. In its simplest terms, it's someone sharing their knowledge and wisdom, and, as Floyd would put it, knowledge about the "how-tos."
>
> Two mentors played major roles in my life but in different ways. At the top of the list was my employer, Gene Hamilton. He was clearly the catalyst for me to develop skills and the how-tos of selling. His philosophical beliefs have been extremely important for me. The second person was a teacher who had an understanding of people and had a vision. He understood who I was. At the right moment, he knew to direct me in a certain way.
>
> Throughout my career I have been a mentor either to salespeople or to managers or business owners. In the last few years, I've become involved with younger people, particularly high school students.
>
> There are times when a mentor might just simply give advice. It may be something as simple as a phone call—"What would you do if . . . ?" You respond with straightforward advice. There is also the other scenario, where you are trying to help a person understand the framework of the fundamentals of what makes people successful. The approach that has worked for me is a very structured, sequential, logical appointment kind of thing where you have a person work through almost a workbook to achieve what you are trying to pass along.
>
> My mentoring sessions have been very structured. I try to bring an individual along in the understanding of how important it

is to plan. We start by setting a five-year plan, reduce it to a one-year plan, then to monthly, weekly, and daily priorities.

If people who have been successful don't assume a responsibility to continue to develop our human resources and sense of entrepreneurship, then who will? I would encourage would-be mentors to look for opportunities and know that they can really help. Mentors do make a difference, whether in the classic sense or whether they are just the individual standing in the "Y" of the road of someone's life.

Being a mentor can be one of the most satisfying experiences you ever have and it will create a sense of well being that you never thought possible. Your contribution to people's lives will live in their hearts forever, and the knowledge you impart to those individuals may very well be passed on for generations. In order to have a successful mentor/protégé relationship, however, there are a number of guidelines that must be followed. We have found these rules, or 16 Laws of Mentoring, provide for a balanced and effective working relationship between the mentor and protégé. In the next chapter, we will introduce you to those laws and explain why they are so important to perpetuating the mentoring lifestyle.

HIGHLIGHTS

❖ While it is often hard to see the value in becoming a mentor, there are six major benefits, including carrying on your legacy and staying sharp.

❖ The most important benefit of mentoring is learning that you get by giving.

❖ Being a mentor can help keep you going when faced with adversity.

❖ Mentors must give their time unselfishly and be committed.

❖ There are eight steps to finding and selecting a protégé that end with you both making a commitment.

❖ Many mentors find that a structured approach toward protégés often works best, but protégés must have a suitable personality for the role.

6

CHAPTER

The 16 Laws of Mentoring

*If you want to be a master, study what the masters have done
before you. Learn to do what they have done—have the guts
to do it—and you will be a master too.*
Jos J. Charbonneau, CSP, CPAE.

We have discussed the benefits of mentoring and shown you how
mentoring can be applied to your daily life and can be instrumental
in helping you reach your goals. We have also taken a detailed look
at what it means to be a protégé and a mentor. Next we showed you
how to go about finding and selecting both a protégé and mentor.
This chapter however, contains the real essence of this entire process.
The 16 Laws of Mentoring represent the distilled knowledge of more
than 30 years of practical experience with mentoring relationships.

Needless to say, it is one thing to acquire a mentor or protégé
and quite another to keep them. The 16 Laws will help you keep
the mentoring relationship going through the ups and downs you
are bound to experience in the pursuit of your life's goals or in an
effort to help another human being.

We have had a number of mentors and protégés over the years.
Through interviews, research, and trial and error, we have discovered
that there are a set number of characteristics that a mentoring relationship must display if it is going to last. We have captured these
traits as a set of guidelines that we call the 16 Laws of Mentoring.

This set of real-world principles should help you as both a protégé and a mentor to keep your mentoring relationships, whether personal or professional, on track and productive. Each law is illustrated by a story submitted by a business friend, colleague, or associate in the hope that its message will help clarify the intent of each law as you see its theme revealed through the experiences of others. We recognize that each story may not relate to your life specifically, but we hope you will acquire a greater understanding of the principles through exposure to these varied experiences of others from all walks of life, which show how the magic of mentoring really works.

1. THE LAW OF POSITIVE ENVIRONMENT

Create a positive environment where potential and motivation are released and options discussed.

It is important that both the mentor and protégé create a positive environment, the type of atmosphere where a person's potential is enhanced and his motivation is increased. A mentor must believe in the protégé even if the protégé doesn't believe in himself. It is the mentor's job to inspire the protégé to think creatively. The protégé needs to be encouraged to accomplish whatever he is capable of. In a positive environment, the protégé will accomplish far more than he could on his own, and often more than he believed was ever possible. Positive energy and compassion must be key elements in the relationship.

Oftentimes our expectations of someone have a lasting, profound impact on behavior. This submission from psychotherapist Judy Tatelbaum, author of *The Courage to Grieve* and *You Don't Have to Suffer*, shows how positive energy and compassion changed the life of one of her patients and, in the process, left a profound impression on the mentor's life as well.

THE AMAZING BENEFITS OF A POSITIVE ENVIRONMENT

As a young social worker in a New York City psychiatric clinic, I was asked to see a 20-year-old woman named Roz who had been

continues

---

concluded

referred to us from another psychiatric facility. It was an unusual referral in that no information was received ahead of her first appointment. I was told to "play it by ear," so to speak, and to figure out what her problems were.

Without a diagnosis to go on, I saw Roz as an unhappy, misunderstood young woman who hadn't been listened to in her earlier therapy. I didn't see her as disturbed, but rather as lonely and misunderstood. She responded positively to having a listener as she shared her feelings. I worked with her to start a life worth living—to find a job, a satisfying place to live, and new relationships. We hit it off well, and she started making important changes in her life right away.

The records from the previous psychiatric facility arrived at least a month after Roz and I had begun our successful work together. Her records were several inches thick, describing several psychiatric hospitalizations. Her diagnosis was: "paranoid schizophrenic," with the comment that she was "hopeless."

That wasn't my experience with Roz, and I never treated her as if she had that "hopeless" diagnosis. (It was a lesson for me to question the value and certainty of future diagnoses.) I did find out a lot about the horrors for Roz of those hospitalizations—of being drugged, isolated, and abused.

First Roz found a job and then a place to live apart from her difficult family. After several months of working together, Roz introduced me to her husband-to-be, a successful businessman. When we completed our therapy, she gave me a gift of a silver bookmark and a note that said, "Thank you for believing me well." I have carried that note with me all the rest of my life to remind me of the stand I take for people.

The effects of believing in someone can be transfiguring, as this story illustrates. It also symbolizes the advantages that can come from making a fresh start. Oftentimes we don't believe in ourselves or that we can do things that actually are within our grasp. It sometimes takes someone else's belief in our abilities to give us the confidence to try.

2. THE LAW OF DEVELOPING CHARACTER

Nurture a positive character by helping to develop not just talent, but a wealth of mental and ethical traits.

You can have the most intelligent, talented person in the world for a protégé, but if that person is ethically insensitive, it is highly unlikely that he or she will be a grand success, regardless of the endeavor. Developing character is an area where a mentor can be particularly helpful to a protégé. A mentor can show a protégé how to deal with extreme setbacks. A mentor should teach a protégé the value of character and demonstrate the downside of unethical behavior. A mentor can help a protégé face his or her fears and build an individual's character, as this submission from Barb Wingfield, president of Wingfield Enterprises in Rushsylvania, Ohio, illustrates.

SLAYING DRAGONS

If I had dreamed of the perfect mentor, my wildest imagination would not have envisioned someone as spectacular as Barbara Braham. I came from a farming community where kids, cows, and corn were the subject of intense reflection. Barbara, on the other hand, presented herself with the grandeur of a European duchess, complete with mink coat; magnificently manicured, painted, long fingernails; and a familiarity with Russian tea rooms. There was nothing superficial about this lady, however. If you were to open your dictionary and look for someone who walks their talk, you would find Barbara's name.

Her gentle way of teaching people to discover the truths in life and business have affected scores of inquiring individuals. One notable example occurred while we were in Washington D.C. together. I saw her compassion and understanding demonstrated one afternoon as she spoke to a former soldier who had just shied away from walking up to the wall of lost names on the Vietnam Memorial. As she skillfully guided him through his fears and apprehensions of this monument to a devastated generation, she encouraged him to rise at dawn and come back and visit it before he left the city. The next day I saw him there, but Barbara did not. He gave me a note to pass along to her. It read, "I slayed the dragon."

Helping someone to overcome their fears and, in the process, increasing the measure of their personal courage is at the core of mentoring. The mentor's actions set the example, and even when we may not realize it, protégés learn the most from the things we show them, not just the things we tell them. Another aspect of developing character is to help protégés become more independent, the focus of the next law.

3. THE LAW OF INDEPENDENCE

Promote autonomy; make the protégé independent of you, not dependent on you.

A mentor should seek to promote autonomy in the protégé. As a mentor, the object is to make the protégé independent of you, not dependent on you. The protégé may need some help, but shouldn't become so dependent on the mentor doing all the thinking that he or she can't function alone. The object is to make protégés' tasks easy enough to encourage them to continue, but hard enough to force them to grow.

We frequently refer to a biblical analogy when we talk about the Law of Independence. If you give a person the gift of a fish, you feed them for a day. If you teach a person how to fish, you feed them for life. In our training programs, the philosophy always has been to teach students first how to fish, then to go out and catch something. There are a lot of people who live near the ocean and own boats and nets but are starving because nobody ever taught them to actually fish. To make people independent of you, you not only have to teach them how but make them do it a few times. You need to make them accountable by applying what you teach them. That's how you encourage independence in a protégé. This submission from Burt Dubin describes how his mentor changed his life and taught him to rely on his own skills and judgment.

THE POWER OF BELIEVING IN SOMEONE

The oscilloscope blipped when it should have zipped. It was a new problem. I'd never encountered it before. I huddled over the electronic test workstation, one of about 30 cubicles in the test cage. The

continues

concluded

technician, more befuddled than I, perceived my quandary. As troubleshooter, I was supposed to know every answer—and I didn't.

A month ago I'd been promoted to my new job over 29 others, and most of them were far more experienced than I. This promotion was over the shop steward's strong objections as well, and he was quite put out because I had prevailed over him with the new work standard I conceived. Young, inexperienced, and not knowing it was impossible, I figured out how to shorten a test and alignment procedure from 45 minutes to 15 minutes, which was shortening it a lot. At first RCA™ was skeptical, and the management brought in a team of engineers to see if I were leaving something out. However, they saw that my new procedure was just as thorough as the old one, and it was three times faster, so they gave it the OK. The company then rewrote the procedure. They tripled production almost overnight.

I was then promoted to a troubleshooter—a very high position for a kid not even shaving yet. Since I conceived this new, shorter process, they figured I could fix the flaws. Little did they know! My boss, Dick Baker, who had previously done all the troubleshooting, took me aside. He showed me the finer points, the esoteric and little-known secrets of isolating electronic problems. He revealed special ways to work with the test equipment. He even shared the psychological fine points of helping a technician in trouble. You had to be sure the techie's self-esteem stayed intact. Dick Baker was my first mentor.

Here I was, up to my ears in confusion, eyebrows knotted, hunched over the millivolt meter, staring at the CRT. I didn't know what to do next. Then I overheard my mentor Dick speaking softly to a techie about two cubicles away. "That young Burt," he said, "understands this process so well, he never has to call on me for help anymore." My heart definitely skipped a beat. Somebody believed in me. My boss believed in me. This boost to my self-esteem was so powerful that I remember it vividly to this day. I stared down the electronic challenge facing me. I dug into my mental resources, my technical know-how, and even my spiritual resources. This challenge wasn't going to lick me. I refused to let it; I was resolute. Licking my lips, focusing like never before, I could almost feel smoke rising from my brain! Then it happened. An intuitive flash. I tried it, and it worked. I had solved the problem. More than that, I manifested a level of competence I never before knew I had. I never again had to call on Dick for help with any problem. He had mentored me, but now he believed in me. That made all the difference.

Believing in your protégé before his or her skills are put to the test is one way to help develop independence. The objective is to help protégés accomplish their goals through enhancing their intellectual, creative, and spiritual abilities.

4. THE LAW OF LIMITED RESPONSIBILITY

Be responsible to them, not for them.

A mentor should not feel as though he or she is responsible for either the protégé's behavior or success. This is because a mentor does not have sufficient control or authority over the protégé to warrant that level of responsibility. You are not the protégé's parent. A mentor is, however, responsible *to* the protégé for doing what he says he will do and giving the best advice and counsel he can.

You are responsible to other people to be the best person you can be, but if you take the relationship too personally and assume responsibility for the how the protégé turns out, you will be exerting too much control over the person and assuming a level of responsibility that can lead to severe frustration.

Conversely, protégés should be careful about becoming too dependent upon a single mentor to secure their careers. A March 1992 article in *American Banker* cites the need for protégés to recognize the fact that their mentor may be as vulnerable as they are within a corporate environment. Kenneth R. Dubuque, then chairman of the Mellon Bank of Maryland, tells his protégés bluntly: "Don't hang your career on me." Protégés should not rely on a single mentor, particularly in industries where mergers and acquisitions are everyday events.

Floyd's cousin is a young man who spent 14 of his 17 years of adult life in prison. While in jail, he developed into quite a good painter. He was having difficulty getting paroled, however, and Floyd went to the parole board hearing to speak on his behalf. When the authorities asked why they should grant the parole, Floyd said, "I believe people go back to prison because they lose hope. I will commit to you and to my cousin that I will be there so things never get hopeless for him." The parole was granted.

As it turned out, Floyd put his cousin through one of his courses. (This was Floyd's "Sweathogs for Life" session—similar to the Sweathogs real estate course but absent the real estate sales training. Students set goals at the beginning that they must reach by the end. For some it is weight loss, for others it's quitting smoking, whatever they think is important.) Floyd's cousin's goal was to sell 10 paintings over the course of the training, and, by the end of the course, he had reached his goal.

He was in Floyd's office afterward and said, "I don't understand it. I hit my goal, but people are griping that the only reason I was able to do it is because I'm your cousin and that you have connections."

Floyd looked at Larry and said, "My whole life has been: You set a goal, stuff happens, but you hit it anyway. Then you set another goal, stuff happens, and you hit it again. That has been the story of my life from day one. But *without any goals and without any achievements, the only thing there is to life is just stuff happening.*"

Floyd got pretty involved in coaching his cousin and offered him a job in the shipping department of his company. He even helped him to establish a line of credit so he could buy a car in order to get back and forth to work. Things seemed to be working out. Then one day the police came. They picked up Larry and took him back to prison. Apparently he had been committing a series of serious crimes during his time off and was using his recently purchased car to prospect new territory.

Floyd was disappointed, but he wasn't devastated. If Floyd had taken full responsibility for what his cousin did with the opportunities he had been given, he probably would never dare offer anyone help again. All he did was to make available certain opportunities to his cousin. He didn't promise to control the outcome.

Mentors are not in the "security business," they are in the "opportunity business." You really can't offer security to people beyond what they are capable of providing for themselves through their own value to society. People either make the most of the opportunities you provide, or they don't. It's not your responsibility what people do with the opportunities.

5. THE LAW OF SHARED MISTAKES

Share your failures as well as your successes.

Being involved in a mentor/protégé relationship means being open, and that means sharing your mistakes and failures as well as your successes. A protégé needs to hear about the errors a mentor made along the way as well as the accomplishments. This lets the protégé appreciate the problems he or she can expect to encounter while pursuing a goal. It is important to share the painful experiences that occur throughout a career. It's not easy to build your own company—we don't think there is anything more difficult. It was really a rude awakening for Terri going from being a top sales producer for Resource Dynamics and the Achievement Group to opening her own company. The overhead, the responsibility, and the time commitment represented an ordeal. In her first year running Sjodin Communications, she was still in graduate school and had gone through all the money she had earned as a sales representative. Terri has always believed her parents have been profound mentors in her life. The following story illustrates how sharing your failures, albeit a bit humiliating, is necessary not only as a protégé but as a mentor as well.

While Terri was going to school on Tuesday and Thursday nights, she was waiting tables Monday, Wednesday, Friday, and Saturday nights and on Sunday morning. That paid for her assistant, who worked out of her home office. Then she worked at her business from 7:30 in the morning until 4:30 in the afternoon. The result of all this work was that she was exhausted, had little money, and faced a mortgage payment that was frightening. If she couldn't pay it, she had nowhere else to go. She was trapped. Terri borrowed $1,000 from her boyfriend, borrowed up to the hilt on her credit cards, and got in deeper and deeper.

It was Christmas, and Terri went to visit her parents. Her mother was in the kitchen and her father was in the garage, where she stopped in to visit. "My dad looked at me and he said, 'Terri Lynn, what has happened to you? I've never seen you look so completely frazzled, and overextended—what are you doing?'" Terri stared back at him, unaware that the pressures on her were so obvious.

"Why don't you just go back to holding down a real job?" asked her father. "Why don't you go back to what you were doing before? Why don't you just go back to sales and working for your old company—you were so good at it."

Terri said, "Dad, just hang in there; I know I can make this happen. Please believe in me." He said, "Well just look at you. You've lost weight, you're pale, and you look sick. Is there anything we can do?"

"No Dad, just hang in there," said Terri.

"We've got to be able to help *some* way," he replied. "Isn't there anything we can do?"

Terri, starting to sound defiant, insisted she didn't need any help. Finally her father said, "Well, can we at least lend you some money?" She wanted to do it all on her own but realized if she didn't ask for help now, she might lose all she had worked for.

"OK," she conceded pitifully but abruptly. "I'll take the money."

With a $1,500 loan from her father, Terri was able to consolidate her business, get back on her feet, and concentrate her energy on her business. She subsequently was able to realize her dream of becoming a professional speaker and an independent entrepreneur and paid back every penny she had borrowed. The point here is not that Terri made a mistake and had to own up to it so much as it is to emphasize that it is important to share your pain and let your protégé know that most people who are successful started out with problems that they later were able to overcome. How were they able to do it? With the help of friends, family, *and mentors* who believed in them during the tough times.

Mentoring is about how to go through and endure painful challenges that emerge as you try to accomplish your goal. If you avoid sharing past and present failures, it creates an unrealistic picture of the price that must be paid to reach any goal. How can a protégé relate to a mentor who never confesses to a mistake? When we discuss what to look for in a mentor, we agree that one of the most important characteristics is to find mentors who have experienced pain. Without pain, they haven't been humbled. And without humility, how can they be good teachers?

In the course of advancing our careers and developing our life management skills there are going to be times when we are left with egg on our face. No one is perfect. In order to learn from these experiences, however, and to keep on course toward our dream, we need to be open about our shortcomings. Both the protégé and the mentor must commit to being open. It is important for the mentor to lead the way in openly sharing mistakes. The mentor must be honest about errors in judgment that will undoubtedly occur during the course of the relationship.

6. THE LAW OF PLANNED OBJECTIVES

Prepare specific goals for your relationship.

We strongly believe in setting goals, in both our personal and business lives. The same is true in a mentoring relationship. In order for the partnership to work, both the mentor and the protégé must agree upon what they want to accomplish together. Your goals should be specific, measurable, and linked to a timetable. Writing goals down can have a tremendous impact on whether or not you accomplish them, as this story from Christopher Frings, Ph.D. and professional speaker from Birmingham, Alabama, shows.

GOALS AND WINNERS

The first time I met coach Bear (Paul William) Bryant, the legendary University of Alabama football coach, he asked me, "Frings, what year did you graduate?" A former student at that renowned institution, I informed him proudly it was in 1961.

"Ah, a very good year!" he said smiling.

For several days that comment stymied me because I didn't really understand what he meant. Forty-eight hours later, a light went on. It was 1961 that his football team had won the National Collegiate Championship the very first time. Every year Bryant had written down that his goal was to win the title. But in 1961 his team actually did it. Over the next 25 years, Alabama would win five more times. Of course, that meant Bryant failed to reach his goal 19 times.

Bryant also had written down a goal—that he recommitted to each year—to win the Southeastern Football Championship title. His team won that 13 times during the same period. Of course that meant Bryant failed to reach his goal 12 times.

Did these failures to achieve so many of his goals make Bryant a failure? Hardly. As coach at one of the nation's leading universities, he won more football games than any coach in the history of the sport.

The truth is, we often don't achieve all our goals. The catch is, if we don't set any goals, we almost certainly will achieve even less.

Winning football championships was Bryant's goal, and it sometimes is hard to relate to the goals of other people. We all need our

continues

---

concluded

own, of course. Bryant used to tell us, "Have goals, have a plan to reach your goals, and stick to your plan."

Bryant was a mentor to many people; some he knew well and others he never even met. But his words are still terrific advice.

Someone once said, "A thing is *not* a thing until it is a thing."

In striving to reach our goals, it is important to keep *the main thing* the main thing. Goal-setting is important. Goal-doing is even more important.

Helping a protégé set goals and establishing specific objectives for the mentor/protégé relationship are both important when evolving into a mentoring lifestyle. The next law has to do with measuring progress toward accomplishing the goals you set.

7. THE LAW OF INSPECTION

Monitor, review, critique, and discuss potential actions. Do not just expect performance without inspection.

Oftentimes a manager will assign a task to an employee and then fail to follow up to see if the person ever accomplished the assignment or even had problems along the way. Some managers don't want to know about the problems encountered by their subordinates. There often is a reluctance on the part of someone in a leadership position to initiate an inspection for fear of making the subordinate uncomfortable. This approach is inappropriate in mentoring.

Young people in particular complain that it makes them feel as though the leadership figure (parent, guardian, teacher, etc.) doesn't trust them. In a way, that is probably true. If you completely trusted someone to accomplish a task exactly as you specified, there probably wouldn't be any need to ask her if she got it done. However, this is an unrealistic expectation when a delegate is experienced, much less in mentoring. The fact is, problems can and do arise even with the simplest undertakings. There may be several solutions for each one of these problems, and one person frequently does not agree with another. This makes life interesting, but it also creates risks.

For a mentor to point the way without reviewing the results is not nearly as effective as both the protégé and mentor discussing the outcome of a plan to determine what happened and why. In the writing profession, few people hone their skills without the constant guidance and feedback of a caring editor. Dick Biggs of Roswell, Georgia, author of *If Life Is a Balancing Act, Why Am I So Darn Clumsy?*, describes in his book how his mentor and editor at the Associated Press coached him along when he was a young reporter trying to learn the craft of writing.

LEARNING TO CARRY YOUR OWN WEIGHT

People have a way of becoming what you encourage them to be—not what you nag them to be. Scudder N. Parker

There is no substitute for ability. Nevertheless, I believe a person's skills are unlikely to reach their full potential without a positive attitude. I also believe a self-confident attitude often makes the difference in securing an opportunity to use one's ability.

Years ago, I left a job as a sportswriter for *The Atlanta Constitution* to enter the Marine Corps. When my four-year enlistment ended, I returned to the *Constitution* to reclaim my former position. I was told that there were no openings but to check upstairs with the Associated Press (AP).

As I got off the elevator, I noticed a crowd of people glaring at me. I had to elbow my way past this throng into a newsroom filled with noisy teletype machines and desks for about 30 people. Oddly enough, there were only four people in the entire place. I approached a man named Lamar Matthews, who happened to be the news editor. I told him I'd been a *Constitution* sportswriter four years ago prior to my Marine duty. "Son," said Matthews, "do you know who those people are out by the elevators?" I didn't. He replied, "That's our striking writers and teletype operators." With all the confidence I could muster, I declared: "Mr. Matthews, it must be my lucky day."

Matthews must have liked my self-confidence because he said, "Biggs, we do need someone to cover the Atlanta Hawks game tonight. Now, you've been away for four years, so just go out there and take some notes. Come back here and we'll help you write your

continues

continued

story." Fortunately, I knew something Matthews didn't know. There was no way they were going to write my story.

The Hawks won at the buzzer in a lengthy game. It was now just five minutes before the copy deadline. There was no way to make it back to the newsroom. I called Matthews, who seemed a bit concerned. I calmly asked, "Are you sitting at a typewriter, sir?" He was, and I replied, "Start typing." I dictated some quick paragraphs from my notes, beat the deadline, and headed back to the AP office.

Matthews and the others were shaking their heads when I walked into the newsroom. "We don't understand how a rookie could do such a professional job after a four-year absence," said Matthews. But remember, I knew something that they didn't know.

I explained that I'd been on embassy duty for the past two years in Europe. I had a lot of spare time. I went to the embassy library and read the great American sportswriters. I even had the audacity to rewrite their columns. I'd visualize myself covering the action. I'd write lead paragraphs for practice.

Obviously, Matthews had underestimated my ability. However, I'm convinced my self-confident attitude, more so than my ability, was what led that AP editor to provide such a gracious opportunity to a "rookie" on that winter night in Georgia.

I mentioned that I got my job as an Associated Press writer due to a strike by the writers and teletype operators. What I didn't say is I never joined the AP union. Naturally, I was branded as a "scab."

Every AP employee had a mail slot. On many occasions, my slot would be filled with negative, anonymous notes about my failure to join the union. Fortunately, my slot would also be filled with positive notes from Lamar Matthews, my news editor.

Matthews was an encourager. He always took the time to review my previous day's work. He would point out my shortcomings, which were many in the beginning, but he would do so in a kind and caring way. More important, Matthews would tell me what I had done right. I still have those reviews, and treasure them like gold. Here are a few examples:

March 7, 1969
"Your copy is better than we normally get from a beginner, but you need a good bit of work. In general, you seem to be straining—trying too hard to write according to some preconceived formula. You'll overcome this if you work at it. Tell it simply, clearly, and smoothly."

continues

concluded

March 20, 1969

"Your copy is becoming much more readable and the style errors called to your attention earlier are being eliminated. You still occasionally use too many words, but generally you're showing good improvement. But I must emphasize the importance of accuracy. Check the facts; use care in rewriting, get it right."

April 8, 1969

"You are to be commended for steady improvement, both in writing and in elimination of style and other mistakes. Please continue to fire away with any questions or let me know if I can help in any way."

April 16, 1969

"Your output last night leaves little doubt about carrying your share of the load. In addition to writing a hefty chunk of the morning copy, I note you did 18 out of 25 evening stories. You've reached the point where speed and volume should be no drawback. Now polish to perfection."

Through his encouraging words, Lamar Matthews empowered me to do better each day despite the nasty notes I received from some of my fellow employees. When I was at the tender age of 23, his encouragement helped me do a tough job in what was often a negative environment.

We consider it a responsibility of the mentor to check the work of the protégé. To simply hand out assignments without following up to see if they were completed or how well they were done will not contribute to success. It is mentors who possess sufficient experience to know whether an action is effective and evaluate performance. It is important for a mentor to find out what the protégé did and how it turned out. The superior mentor does more than just spout textbook truisms—he or she gets involved in the life of the protégé.

8. THE LAW OF TOUGH LOVE

The participants acknowledge the need to encourage independence in the protégé.

The law of tough love is included because there comes a time in most mentor/protégé relationships when the protégé begins to become more dependent on the mentor than may be healthy. The fact that the mentor is placed in a role of guiding and directing the protégé tends to develop an attitude in the latter that, if unchecked, can be counterproductive.

Most relationships create an atmosphere of mutual dependence, which is necessary. The mentor/protégé relationship, by its nature, tends to be somewhat more weighted toward the protégé's dependence on the mentor than the other way around. However, the mentor must evaluate whether the protégé's reliance on him is becoming exaggerated. If it is, it may be the time to administer a little "tough love," meaning the mentor has to give the protégé a little shove in the direction of self-reliance and independence. Sometimes it means pushing the protégé to achieve more than he thought he could with the resources at his disposal.

When encouraging someone to do more than he or she initially wants to do, or feels can be done, the mentor will create some stress in the relationship, so there are risks involved. But the thing to keep in mind is that the main purpose of the union is to foster the protégé's growth and accomplishment. Gentle encouragement is the best tool with which to accomplish this, as the following story from consultant Millie Jarrett demonstrates.

AWAKENING THE WILL TO WIN

Reggie Jackson has given the most perfect definition of a great manager and mentor. "A great manager has a knack for making us think we are better than we think we are. He forces us to have a good opinion of ourselves. He lets us know he believes in us. He makes us get more out of ourselves. And once we learn how good we really are, we never settle for anything less than our very best."

For 21 years, I was fortunate to have this kind of mentor, which made a tremendous difference in my life and in the lives of many others. George Smith, former sales manager, believed in me when I didn't believe in myself. He continuously encouraged me to realize many goals—one step at a time. When I was ready to give up, he used "tough love" for the final challenge to put me over the top. The following story is a typical example.

My first major sales incentive contest was for a Greek Islands cruise. Only the top five personal producers and top five organiza-

continues

concluded

tional producers in North America could win. Smith told me that if I got 20 "personal" orders during the three-week contest I would have a good chance of winning. Naturally, I got 20. He said I would have a better chance, of course, with 25 orders. So I got 25 orders. He then told me I could cinch this wonderful trip with 35 orders. He kept saying, "you *can*. You *can*." Two days before the deadline, I had five cancellations. Working day and night in 101-degree temperature with no air conditioning in my car was becoming unbearable. I was hot, I was tired, and I was discouraged. I wanted to quit. I called my mentor for consolation. Thankfully, I didn't get it. For the first time, my mentor used "tough love." He told me I had to keep going; that I couldn't give up now. I hung up the phone and started to cry. After recovering, I set to work replacing the five cancellations. I ended the contest with 41 orders. Oh yes. It was an unforgettable cruise. And I won the contest every year after that, too.

The protégé will take comfort in knowing he or she has a mentor upon whom to rely for advice and understanding. Sometimes a mentor can make the protégé feel secure. But the point of mentoring is growth, not comfort, though this may often be a side benefit. Thus, when a protégé has attained the goal for which he or she originally sought the mentor's help, or if it becomes clear the protégé has now acquired the skills of the mentor, it may be time for the protégé to establish another goal and possibly select another mentor.

Often the protégé will be reluctant to initiate severing the relationship. Those of you who have been protégés know the feeling of wanting to stay in the nest. Even within a long-term mentoring relationship, it is important for the mentor to keep in mind that the protégé's comfort is not paramount. The mentor shouldn't be afraid to shake up the protégé every once in a while to avoid his or her becoming unduly dependent.

9. THE LAW OF SMALL SUCCESSES

Use a stepping-stone process to build on accomplishments and achieve great success.

The one-step-at-a-time approach is the premise behind spaced training programs. They give people only as much help and information as they can digest. Later, they apply it so they can build a foundation of experience on which to continue growing.

When Floyd was a young man just out of the Navy he was working as a milkman making a $1,000 a month. But he dreamed about making a $1,000 a week. He kept thinking about how, instead of making $1,000 a month, he could make the same amount in a single week. He knew he wasn't going to do it delivering milk. So he started looking around for something else. He found it in real estate where he went from $12,000 a year, or $1,000 a month, to $1,000 a week.

While Floyd was in real estate making $1,000 a week, he saw a speaker who was being paid even more than he was. He thought to himself, "I wonder if I could make $1,000 a day like he does?" Floyd used his foundation of success in real estate to become a real estate speaker where he began earning a $1,000 a day to give talks.

Seeing the success he was having as a speaker, Floyd asked, "What if I could train other people to do what I do, then have them do it for me? We could share in the rewards together, and I could make a $1,000 an hour." That is how the Floyd Wickman Courses training company was born, which now has trainers throughout the country. Floyd's organization was built on a foundation in stepping stone increments.

The success of the protégé should be accomplished in small increments too, and both the mentor and protégé should approach the objectives of the mentoring relationship one step at a time.

10. THE LAW OF DIRECTION

It is important to teach by giving options as well as direction.

This law is born from the belief that usually there is more than one way to accomplish something. It also results from the fact that nobody likes being told what to do all the time. The mentor/protégé relationship is not that of a master and slave. It is a voluntary relationship. The mentor should not become so focused on his path that he can't see any other way of doing things. A highly autocratic style in which the mentor dictates how the protégé should solve every problem is simply inappropriate. The mentor is a resource for the protégé. His or her length of experience in a given area provides a background of proven techniques for a given list of problems. However, every situation is different, and no two individuals are the same. Therefore it is important for the mentor to adopt a style in which options are offered to the protégé as a way to encourage her to try new approaches. The mentor might say, "This is how I did it, but let me give you some options so you can do it in different ways. You don't have to follow the exact same path that I took." The mentor should allow the protégé to choose the path that is best for her.

At the same time, the law of direction provides for the mentor to be very explicit about what the protégé should do if she is confused about her next step. Often in life we find ourselves in situations we would never have anticipated. When we ask ourselves why, the mentor may feel it is appropriate to give us a clear pointer in a different direction.

A young man who was one of our first trainees ended up taking the Dale Carnegie course with Floyd back in the mid-to-late 60s. They had a sales presentation contest at Dale Carnegie, and Floyd lost to the trainee. Floyd did win the prize for being the student who did the most for the class, for which he was very proud.

Some 30 years later, Floyd had built a large company and was training up to 10,000 students a year, while at the same time speaking 200 days. The trainee who started out with Floyd, meanwhile, was earning about the same amount of money he was 30 years earlier. They had kept in touch, and one day he said to Floyd, "I don't understand it. Why, when we started out the same, are you up here, and I'm down there?" Floyd looked at him and said, "The only difference between you and me is that from the very beginning, I believed I could do it. You didn't." Floyd then gave him an assignment. He said, "I want you to go out and buy the book, *As a Man Thinketh* by James Allen. Read a passage from it three times a day for the next 30 days."

The man did as Floyd suggested, and not surprisingly, his income tripled in a relatively short period. He became a protégé of Floyd's and currently owns his own subsidiary of Floyd Wickman Courses called The Master Resource. He recently bought a house down the street from Floyd on the canal, and the two go boating together.

11. THE LAWS OF RISK

A mentor should be aware that a protégé's failure may reflect back upon him . A protégé should realize that a mentor's advice will not always work.

There is some risk as we assume the roles of mentor and protégé. For a mentor, the risk is failure of the protégé, which reflects poorly on the mentor. People might say, "Well, you couldn't be a very good mentor because your protégé performed badly," or, possibly, "broke a law." All this will reflect on you; once you sponsor a protégé, there is visibility and exposure, which entails public identification between you two. This may carry considerable social and political implications. Imagine a situation where the mentor invites the protégé to a cocktail party and the protégé proceeds to have one too many. Not only does this limit the opportunities the protégé could have taken advantage of at the party, but it makes the mentor look bad for having invited him in the first place.

However, as a protégé, you have to be willing to accept that the reality that a mentor's advice may not always work. He or she is basically sharing knowledge, based on his or her best educated guess. Let us imagine that you tell your mentor that you are negotiating a contract and ask her how to position yourself. Suppose she says, "Well, if I were you, I would play hardball, and I wouldn't give an inch. I would remain steadfast in order to get the deal I really wanted." So you take your mentor's advice. You remain calm, firm, and tough during negotiations. But, guess what? You lose the deal! You might resent it if you took the tough stance because your mentor "told you to." Well, no one is perfect, and your mentor's advice was really her best guess. You run a risk every time you take your mentor's advice that the solution will not work in that situation. There are risks for both mentor and protégé, and you should face those risks together.

12. THE LAW OF MUTUAL PROTECTION

Commit to cover each other's backs. Maintain privacy. Protect integrity, character, and the pearls of wisdom you have shared with one another.

When you enter into a mentoring relationship, you are taking a risk. This is a process to spur change, which makes results sometimes unpredictable. Mistakes will be made, emotions will become involved, and people may get exasperated when results don't measure up to expectations. All this is natural. Having an experienced mentor involved is intended to reduce frustration and slant results toward success whenever a new challenge is undertaken. But this is real life, and things don't always work out the way we plan them.

In the course of this adventure, both the protégé and mentor must realize that they are on the "same team," to use a sports analogy. The failure or inadequacy of one reflects on the other. Therefore, it is in the interests of each of them to protect the other's reputation. If the behavior of either your mentor or your protégé is so egregious that you need to tell someone else about that person's shortcomings, you may want to sever the relationship and find someone with whom you feel more compatible. Otherwise, privacy and confidentiality are the rule.

When going over the 16 Laws of Mentoring, it is important to discuss this aspect of the relationship and make an open and clear commitment to this principle *before* someone becomes embarrassed and has their feelings hurt.

Another, more subtle, aspect to this law revolves around the freedom that two people achieve when they trust each other. If you have to worry that people are going to repeat everything you say as soon as they get out the door, you tend to be more guarded in your comments. It takes more work to screen every word, and the relationship loses spontaneity.

The key word here is trust, and you both have to make a determined effort to earn each other's confidence by respecting the privacy of the relationship and, in some cases, actively defending the other person's reputation. One gift that protégés say is among the most important a mentor can bequeath to his protégé is that of believing in him, often when the protégé doesn't believe in himself. An ideal way to express that belief is by defending someone should they ever come under attack. In the following submission, quality control expert Ron Bourque of Windham, New Hampshire, recalls the time his mentor came to the rescue when he was publicly criticized.

DEFENDING YOUR PROTÉGÉ, SUPPORTING YOUR MENTOR

Back in the early 80s, I was working in the supplier certification program of a large computer company. My job was to lead teams of engineers into supplier facilities and perform detailed assessments to determine their capabilities to consistently produce high-quality, reliable products. The assessments were usually referred to as "audits" with all the negative connotations associated with these activities.

I had decided to revamp the assessment process to a more cooperative approach. I would try the new approach in Albuquerque, New Mexico, a site which had been notoriously uncooperative in the past. My boss thought I was crazy. He told me if it didn't work that I need not come back.

It worked so well that before long I became the preferred lead auditor, and everyone was trying to learn how to do it this new way. About a year later, I was participating in an organization called GOAL/QPC. Its mission was to help local companies improve competitiveness. Supplier issues quickly came to the forefront as a common problem, so I offered to share my approach to supplier qualification. We agreed on a date, and my presentation was well received.

One of the people in the audience that day was Jack Newcomb, a professor at MIT's Center for Advanced Engineering Studies. MIT had just published Dr. W. Edwards Deming's book, *Quality, Productivity and Competitive Position* (CAES/MIT, Cambridge, MA, 1982). MIT was running a series of workshops featuring Dr. Deming and several supporting speakers, so Jack asked if I would like to give my presentation.

Despite several senior managers at my firm becoming ruffled when they heard I was on the program, my supervisor and the new division vice president of quality intervened on my behalf.

The big day approached, and I was nervous. Everyone else had impressive pedigrees. Some were internationally renowned, others had Ph.Ds. I was a lowly senior lead engineer with a bachelor of science degree.

Jack was emceeing the conference and introduced the speakers. I will never forget my introduction. He had nothing to work with, but he made me feel like a million dollars without telling a single fib. Because of the great introduction, the audience was receptive. I resolved not to let Jack down.

continues

concluded

Something must have worked because Jack invited me to speak at two more conferences. His introductions were always the most encouraging words I ever heard. I'm still grateful. But I learned something from him, which was even more important. We became friends and would occasionally have lunch or dinner together. I was always amazed at how he would interrupt our important discussions to make a waitress, who might have been doing a poor job, feel good about herself. Of course, our service would improve immediately. Jack had formed the habit of seeing people *not as they are, but as they were capable of becoming.*

Another benefit of participating in these workshops was getting to know Dr. Deming. I had already met and had dinner with him. On a personal level, I found him to be gentle; he reminded me of my maternal grandfather. He had a reputation, however, of being tactless and abrupt. I began to realize that the impatience he displayed was caused by his understanding of the sheer magnitude of waste from our management practices and the unnecessary job losses which resulted.

When I once made this point, I was told I could afford to be understanding because I never had been publicly embarrassed by him. Actually, I had. Once in San Diego, Dr. Deming stood up in the middle of my presentation and said, "That's not true!" Many people have no idea what if feels like to get called a liar in front of several hundred people by the world renowned "Mr. Quality." I'm not one of them. What could I use for a comeback? Again, Jack Newcomb, my mentor, came to the rescue. Dr. Deming had a problem hearing me, and he had misunderstood what I had said. But once Jack helped him understand, he apologized, and I continued.

Perhaps the greatest benefit I received from Jack was the self-confidence I developed from the faith he and my other mentors had in me. Eventually, I developed several presentations, and my company sent me all over the world, from Singapore to Israel, and many places in between, to present them. This could never have happened without the support of my mentors—including Dr. Deming. I doubt I will be in a position to repay them, but I can try to do for others what they did so well for me.

People remember it when you stand up for them, and they take it as a belief in their (sometimes undemonstrated) abilities when you defend them. It is worth noting that even though Ron was embarrassed on one occasion by the preeminent leader in his field, he didn't take offense. Instead he cultivated this revered individual into another mentor!

13. THE LAW OF COMMUNICATION

The mentor and the protégé must balance listening with delivering information.

One of the secrets to success in a mentoring relationship is to use good communication techniques. The missing link in most mentor/protégé unions is what psychologists call *reflection*. This means whether the mentor or protégé is speaking, the listener needs to mirror back the message—both the thoughts and emotions.

According to Gerald Goodman, associate professor of psychology at UCLA, the use of reflection is the "missing link" in mentoring and many other types of communications. Most people aren't aware, however, of the power they can exert in improving communications when they employ reflection, Goodman writes in *The Talk Book*.

Use of reflection begins with empathy, says Goodman. After focusing on the other person, you state back what you heard her say but in a condensed form. When a mentor employs this technique with a protégé, it gives the protégé the feeling that she has been heard and her feelings understood.

Richard Tyre, of the Uncommon Individual Foundation, said in a June 30, 1992, *Wilmington News Journal* article that the key to success in mentoring—or any other sincere relationship—is the use of reflection. "If you practice this, people believe you're sensitive, insightful, and wise, and they come away from a conversation with a sense of confidence they can use whatever power they have to the best of their ability."

14. THE LAW OF EXTENDED COMMITMENT

The mentoring relationship extends beyond the typical 9–to–5 business day and/or traditional workplace role or position.

The point of mentoring is not only to pass on information but also to inspire. A kind word, an understanding ear, a sympathetic response from someone who has known and overcome the pain of struggling toward an important goal—these kinds of messages are often more important than specific problem-solving techniques. The timing of these words of encouragement is just as important as the actual content. If someone is hurt and discouraged, telling them to wait until you can get back to them in a few days isn't going to do them any good.

The relationship between mentor and protégé can be structured any way that is convenient for both. We have found, however, that it works best if the mentor and protégé try to be as flexible as possible. Even if you both are employed at the same company, the commitment to support one another should extend beyond normal business hours. This can be a delicate area, and the protégé must respect the mentor's privacy. But the mentor in turn should go the extra mile and be available to the protégé at the time help is needed—not next week, or next month when it might not matter anymore. Being accessible is part of mentoring, and the success of your relationship will depend to some extent on how accessible you are to each other. This of course applies to most other relationships as well!

The following story from Ken Wallace, of Carbondale, Illinois shows how putting someone off until some unspecified time in the future sets up a dynamic that undermines sharing and communication.

TOMORROW NEVER COMES

When children ask you to do something for them, when do they want it done? Right now, right? Have you ever responded to a child who has asked you to do something with words like, "Not now, I'm too busy," or "Later," or "In a while?"

When my children were little, I developed the unfortunate habit of responding to their requests for my time and attention with a single word: "Tomorrow." I didn't realize how frequently I was saying this until one day when we finished shopping in our local grocery. We were waiting in the check-out line when I gave in and bought my daughter, Rachel, a package of *my* favorite candy, Lifesavers™.

As we were driving home, Rachel sat in the back of the car eagerly unwrapping her package of Lifesavers. She fully intended to eat

continues

concluded

as many of them as she could before we got home. Her usual approach to candy was to eat them all at once.

Suddenly the air in the car was filled with the sweet aroma of my childhood. I began to salivate. I couldn't help myself. I also couldn't stop the next words that slipped out of my mouth: "Rachel, may I have a Lifesaver?" I asked, anticipating the next part of the conversation to revolve around my choice of which flavor

But what do you think she said to me? "TOMORROW!"

The moment she said it, I realized that, with a single word repeated over a period of time, I had created a reality in my children's lives that said, "Daddy will be our daddy and do daddy things with us—tomorrow." I also realized that if I ever were going to be a father to my children in the way they needed, I would have to be one today. Because tomorrow never comes . . .

In many cases, being someone's mentor can make the difference in her life between success and failure. When a mentor is able to see a person as what they could be rather than what they are today, it can have a remarkable impact on her self-image and performance. Sometimes taking a little extra effort that may extend beyond what we would consider ordinary and customary can reinforce in the protégé's mind that she is a valuable person with important qualities, as illustrated by Devon Hansen's (president of Inner Dynamics Consulting) recollection of her experiences with her mentor Rosita Perez.

A GIFT FROM THE HEART

When most people think of a mentor, they imagine a master teacher who helps others by taking them under their wings of wisdom, teaching them to fly. Once they can fly, the teacher may no longer be needed. In my imagination, soaring to success was a thought that quickly flew by. To spread my wings and fly with success I would need more than a few flying lessons. I would need extended commitment from a mentor who gave me ample time to trust the teacher before I could discover the lesson.

continues

continued

When I first met my mentor, Rosita Perez, I couldn't begin to comprehend how her extended commitment to me would impact and inspire me to make major changes in my life. Rosita would become the only person who ever took time to believe in me so I could begin to believe in myself. My motivation to succeed was buried underneath the agony I was harboring from past experiences.

To understand my need for extended commitment, you must first understand me. I was the anguished victim of a shocking betrayal and conspiracy by the judicial system. During a brief preliminary hearing concerning my divorce and custody of my children, my whole world changed. With less than a blink from the judge's eye, with no supporting evidence, he placed my three small children in foster care and ordered me out of my home by the end of the evening. The judge reasoned he wanted to give the parents time to see who could provide a better lifestyle for the children. I was clearly at a disadvantage. I was a housewife with no education, but my husband was a prominent doctor.

As the sun began to set, I began my journey to a helpless, hopeless, and homeless life. With no supportive family or friends to help, I drifted city streets for the next two years. I had to associate with social outcasts and was an easy target for night stalkers. I soon learned no one was safe in these dark corners. Eventually, I was placed into a low-income housing project where I would reside for eight more years. My 10-year experience tortured my soul, twisted my faith, and drained me of hope.

I wanted to escape life in the projects but lacked the know-how. When I learned about a "How to Start Your Own Speaking Business" seminar, I temporarily put away my hardened attitude and the chip on my shoulder and attended. I needed a lot of help, but during the seminar I learned how to set goals and take steps towards positive networking.

I began attending Ohio Speaker Forum (OSF) meetings to obtain skills to become a professional speaker. Eventually, I was invited to speak at an OSF meeting. I was terrified! I spent most of the morning in the restroom doing deep breathing and throwing up! I had never used a microphone and I was not about to start with "real" speakers watching me. I just stood up on the platform and belted out my message from my heart, soul—and trembling knees. Little did I know that on this day magic was about to happen.

continues

continued

I am learning disabled and unable to prepare for a talk. I work strictly from audience energy. Terror blocked me this day until I felt a strong pull from a beautiful woman with large dark eyes and black silky hair. Oddly, she was wearing a colorful flower in her hair. Her eyes told me she was rooting for me. Her energy sent me a soothing message as if to say everything was going to be okay. Much to my surprise, she was right. The audience gave me a roaring standing ovation. I was totally disarmed with emotion. I felt my tears begin to surface. What was I to do? The streets taught me to harden and hide my feelings. But, where could I hide?

Frantically, my eyes searched for the woman with the flower in her hair. When I spotted her, she was standing with her arms opened wide holding an invitation with my name on it. I bolted straight to her for safety. The love coming from her embrace was like a warm blanket comforting my wounded soul. Few words were spoken, but immediately I knew the experience was in my heart forever. Later, I learned the woman was Rosita Perez, a well-known and respected professional speaker. The flower in hair was her trademark, her inner warmth was mentor excellence.

Rosita contacted me by letter and became my mentor who provided honest feedback and focused on my strengths as she nurtured my weaknesses. Keep in mind, I had no professional training and I was still street tough and very defensive. I didn't realize how my intensity could affect and often threaten people. I desperately needed an extended commitment from Rosita because it gave me the necessary time to acquire professional skills and allowed me to recover the gentleness I had lost. The streets had taught me never to reach out for help. Guess what? I didn't have to ask. Rosita automatically knew what I needed and willingly offered herself and her time to me.

At first, I was guarded and unable to trust Rosita's interest in me. I had been hurt and used by so many people. Why would she be any different? Because my mentor gave her gift of extended commitment, I was eventually able to establish a trusting relationship with her. I was able to let her in my heart and believe she really cared for me. Rosita never once judged me for my past experiences. She always focused on the good in me, devoting many years of mentoring advice and support. She offered me patience as I worked to regain my personal dignity. She took time to nurture my professional and personal insecurities. Rosita never shamed me when I

continues

concluded

would take the risk to tell her about my many fears of success. She called up the passion in me to make a difference in this world. I set out to do just that!

My mentor's extended commitment gave me the necessary support I needed to succeed professionally as a speaker, published author, and consultant. Extended commitment from her also helped me seek out justice in my personal life. With my newfound energy, fueled by the recognition of extreme injustice, I single-handedly challenged the system that put me on the streets. With the odds stacked against me, I reached victory and regained custody of my children. My life story is being made into a Hollywood movie for television.

I am grateful and I thank God for my many blessings. I especially thank my mentor for her gift of extended commitment to me, the one present I will cherish for a lifetime. In my eyes, Rosita is a star because a star is truly one who shines. Rosita shined her light on me even during my darkest hours. She took time to teach me that when you have a true sense of purpose, success will follow. Her extended commitment gave me time to find success by turning my failures inside out.

15. THE LAW OF LIFE TRANSITION

As a mentor, when you help a protégé enter the next stage of his life or career, you will enter the next stage of yours.

There have been several studies on the effect that working with protégés has on a mentor's self-image and sense of fulfillment. While we have found from personal experience that mentoring enhances our sense of self-worth and generally makes us feel good about ourselves, this positive effect also has been documented by social scientists.

In a March 22, 1993, issue of the *Journal of Management*, Belle Rose Ragins and John L. Cotton refer to studies of others dating back as early as the 1960s in which researchers found that mentoring is critical to obtaining a sense of contribution to future generations. Without experiencing this sense of helping future generations, an individual is likely to become stagnant and displays trouble moving on to the next stage of life.

The research also found that mentoring is a "crucial activity" during the midlife of a person's career if the individual wants to retain a sense of challenge and keep growing. Without a challenge, the individual begins to question the value of work. This hesitation in commitment is often accompanied by a decrease in organization, involvement, satisfaction, and performance! "Mentoring can help the individual move through this career transition by providing a sense of purpose and direction," note the authors, as the following story shows.

RIGHTSIZING YOURSELF

An acquaintance of ours named Steve, a man in his early 50s, had worked for a major corporation but was caught in a "downsizing" initiative sweeping the industry. After 26 years at the same firm, like so many people today, he was laid off and forced to find some other way to earn a living. Unlike many, he was given a year's severance pay and early retirement. But Steve didn't feel ready to retire nor did he relish accepting the reduction in income that would result from such a decision. Finding another job proved to be a near impossibility. There was a glut of middle management, all scrambling over each other for the same positions.

One of Steve's hobbies, however, was refurbishing cars. Through a shared interest, he met a young man who had started his own automotive refurbishing business. Steve started working with this young fellow, and they both were able to help each other. The young man needed the management and business experience that Steve had developed through the years. Steve, however, needed the young man's enthusiasm. The protégé was so pumped up about his industry that he gave Steve the fire and vigor he needed to approach a new career at that stage in his life.

Steve's wife says he is now happier than he was at his old job, has more energy, and looks forward to going to work every day. He did take an initial step backward in income, but after a couple of years, he now is close to making what he earned in his former position with the corporation. If it hadn't been for taking on a protégé and helping him with his business, Steve would have had a lot more trouble with the life transition he was forced to face.

As a mentor, when you help a protégé enter the next stage of his or her career, you will lubricate the complex mental/emotional mechanism that permits you to glide forward toward the next stage of your own life. There are many areas in which you are very gifted. Consider sharing these gifts with a protégé. You might help someone with his or her spiritual, financial, athletic, family, or other objectives—areas where your knowledge and experience could make the difference between someone's success or failure. It's one of the best gifts you can give someone. Serving as someone's mentor also may encourage you to seek a relationship with another who can share life's pearls of wisdom with you.

16. THE LAW OF FUN

Make mentoring a wonderful experience—laugh, smile, and enjoy the process.

The mentoring process should be a superlative experience. You have the opportunity to make it as much fun as you want. Nothing says we can't have fun while we are learning. All work and no play is not the way to enhance a relationship—with a mentor or anyone else. When two people are involved in the mentoring process, it becomes an enriching part of their lives, and that helps make it fun. It is a unique, interesting bond that relieves life's more tedious aspects. Life shouldn't be the same day in and day out.

We have conducted interviews with numerous mentors and protégés and each has shared with us the observation that as the relationship evolves and matures, it really creates opportunities to have fun. You can attend events together that are related to the subject of interest, such as conferences and seminars. You can meet for lunch, go horseback riding, or just sit around with your families and talk about a few of the things you have done together.

Life should be a pleasurable experience. One of our friends, Ms. Suzie Detro, says, "I don't care what we do, as long as we're having fun." When challenged about what some might question is a naive attitude, she says, "Well, why wouldn't I say that? Fun is the best thing to have!" Ironically, it's true—fun is the best thing to have. What else is better? It is the best thing so it should be part of your philosophy of life.

You wake up each day with the hope that it is going to be happy, healthy, enjoyable, dazzling, and unique, filled with a wonderful experience or a wonderful insight that will carry through to the next day. That's what makes life invigorating. If you are having fun, your relationships stay fresh and dynamic. Your mentor will want to keep meeting with you and feeding you pearls of wisdom if a good portion of time you spend together is fun—a positive, healthy, happy experience.

You now have a good idea of what the 16 Laws of Mentoring are and should have a feel for how to apply them in your ongoing relationships with mentors and protégés. Make the effort to review them together regularly so you both stay on track. They are at the very heart of the mentoring lifestyle and have been proven over the years to allow the mentor/protégé relationship to keep going. They are the result of much trial and error and are a crucial element in the final secret. (On the following page, we summarize them all.)

Next we will address the most common questions people have about mentoring, including problems that may arise. We will tell you what these mean and present several options for overcoming them. We will also hear from people who have been willing to share their heartfelt mentoring experiences.

HIGHLIGHTS

❖ The 16 Laws of Mentoring are intended to assure the long-term stability of the relationship between the mentor and protégé.

❖ The 16 Laws should be reviewed by both parties before committing to a formal mentor/protégé relationship. Both sides should understand and agree to the same rules.

SUMMARY OF THE 16 LAWS OF MENTORING

1. The Law of Positive Environment

Create a positive environment where potential and motivation are released and options discussed.

2. The Law of Developing Character

Nurture a positive character by helping to develop not just talent, but a wealth of mental and ethical traits.

3. The Law of Independence

Promote autonomy; make the protégé independent of you, not dependent on you.

4. The Law of Limited Responsibility

Be responsible to them, not for them.

5. The Law of Shared Mistakes

Share your failures as well as your successes.

6. The Law of Planned Objectives

Prepare specific goals for your relationship.

7. The Law of Inspection

Monitor, review, critique, and discuss potential actions. Do not just expect performance without inspection.

8. The Law of Tough Love

The participants acknowledge the need to encourage independence in the protégé.

9. The Law of Small Successes

Use a stepping-stone process to build on accomplishments and achieve great success.

10. The Law of Direction

It is important to teach by giving options as well as direction.

11. The Laws of Risk

A mentor should be aware that a protégé's failure may reflect back upon him. A protégé should realize that a mentor's advice will not always work.

12. The Law of Mutual Protection

Commit to cover each other's backs. Maintain privacy. Protect integrity, character, and the pearls of wisdom you have shared with one another.

13. The Law of Communication

The mentor and the protégé must balance listening with delivering information.

14. The Law of Extended Commitment

The mentoring relationship extends beyond the typical 9–to–5 business day and/or traditional workplace role or position.

15. The Law of Life Transition

As a mentor, when you help a protégé enter the next stage of his life or career, you will enter the next stage of yours.

16. The Law of Fun

Make mentoring a wonderful experience—laugh, smile, and enjoy the process.

7

CHAPTER

Questions and Comments about Mentoring

Sometimes, part of the responsibility of having a mentor is knowing when you have outgrown each other and realizing when it's time to move on. Michael Jeffreys

We have carefully reviewed the 16 Laws of Mentoring and have gone into detail about how to avoid problems when establishing a mentor/protégé relationship. As we all know, however, problems are a part of life we never can seem to escape.

When we are in the field and delivering our training and development seminars on mentoring, we invariably get questions at the end of the sessions. Usually they have to do with obstacles that people have had to contend with as they attempted to build their mentoring relationships. Be aware that there are going to be hurdles in developing your personal mentoring lifestyle but, like everything else, it gets easier with practice. Mentoring is relatively simple, but not necessarily easy. There is a difference. When something is simple, you can look at it and it makes sense because it is logical. You can see the plan. Just because it is not complicated doesn't mean it's easy to accomplish. Since mentoring involves a human relationship, it can get sticky.

All human relationships include some form of conflict. There are more potential conflicts and issues in mentoring than we can list, but we are going to address the ones most frequently discussed by people who have tried it. All these issues can be resolved with good communication and a commitment to work through the conflicts.

THE EIGHT MOST COMMONLY ASKED QUESTIONS ABOUT MENTORING

1. What Should I Do If I Can't Find a Mentor?

Some people may have had a mentor—perhaps even more than one—or attempted a mentoring relationship in the past, but alas, none has worked. Your first relationship or mentoring experience may not work; maybe the second one won't either. It may take the third or the fourth attempt before you find a long-term mentor. If you truly want a mentor, you may have to keep trying if the first couple of attempts don't take. The 16 Laws of Mentoring should help you to avoid common problems and reasons why some mentoring relationships fail. So you don't repeat the same mistakes, review the 16 Laws to see where your relationships are faltering. These laws emerged out of numerous failed attempts at sustaining mentor/protégé relationships. They work, and you should follow them.

If you can't find a mentor, it is possible you may not be trying hard enough. To leverage your efforts, try narrowing your search. Look for someone who already has had a mentor. Statistics show that those who have had mentors themselves are generally much more willing to mentor someone else. One of your prequalifying questions might be, "Were you ever a protégé to someone in the past?"

Also, look for people who are at or beyond the midpoint in their careers. These individuals typically are more motivated to become mentors. Midcareer professionals who have been mentored before are by far the most likely to agree to become your mentor. Keep looking and keep asking, and confine your search to people who meet these criteria.

Often people will ask, "Doesn't the mentor seek out and actually select the protégé?" Some research suggests that this is true, but there is also evidence supporting the perception that the protégé may also initiate a mentoring relationship. Richard McCloskey, president of Mentoring Systems, Inc., a firm that specializes in initiating mentor programs within the insurance industry, says that most potential mentors must be *sold* on participating. The truth is that sometimes the mentor selects the protégé and sometimes it is the other way around.

2. What If the Mentor or Protégé Doesn't Follow Through?

Your first step is to meet with your partner and talk about the problem. You have prequalified each other and have agreed to form a relationship, yet there is no following through. Can anything be done? If one person notices the impasse, undoubtedly the other person is aware of it too. You both must commit to communicate better and to create a more defined structure for your relationship. That will set a precedent. You have to face the issue head on and not opt for the more comfortable alternatives of proceeding defensively or avoiding each other and letting the relationship gradually fade to black. Be decisive.

Once you have met, shared your grievances, and opened up communications, the relationship still may not be progressing. Even though you tried to define your roles better, it just isn't happening. If this occurs, then it probably is time to dissolve the association. This particular mentoring relationship isn't working, so just get out of it. It's that simple. There are no requirements to continue. This is a voluntary union, and both parties should be involved because they want to be.

If you want to end it, you don't necessarily have to have a formal "breakup." If you are a protégé, you can say that you are moving on to another area of specialization and have found someone more appropriate to help you. Perhaps you might add that you would like to touch base with your mentor from time to time in order to check out an idea with him. Just let the relationship naturally dissolve, but do it openly and without hurting the other's feelings.

If you are a mentor, you can say that you think it is time for the person to move on to someone with a greater level of specialization. Perhaps you don't have as much time to dedicate now, but you will always be there to lend an ear, provide a lead to an information source, or offer direction. You could say, "I don't have anything else to offer you. I have given you all I know, and now I think it's time to move on. I will always be here if you need to talk." Try to direct the protégé to someone else.

If you think the mentor's advice is not sound, or the mentor doesn't do something that he or she promised, remember that a mentoring relationship is always voluntary. In other words, you can't discipline your mentor. Even if you tried, it wouldn't work. If the mentor isn't following through with things he or she promised to do, then you need to find someone else who will. This relationship is supposed to be a graceful, mutually interesting, fun, and upbeat experience, so blaming each other for failures is not an acceptable alternative.

When you have problems, again, be sure to review the 16 Laws of Mentoring. These set the standards for how to manage a lasting relationship. The 16 Laws allow for a lot of openness and result in empowered partners, so follow them to stay on the right track.

3. What If My Company Assigns Me a Mentor Who Doesn't Really Help Me?

A number of companies have initiated formal mentoring programs and are structured enough to have assigned mentors to lower-level individuals, but often there is no mechanism in place to monitor whether or not the relationship is working. These "contract marriages" sometimes are helpful, but they remove the important ingredient of personal choice in selecting a mentor or protégé, so the participants aren't as enthusiastic as they otherwise would be. The types of concerns we hear about go something like this: "My company has a mentor program, but it didn't work for me. They assigned me to someone I don't think really wants to be involved. My close friend got someone who was really good, but my mentor didn't do anything."

Another variation of this theme is: "I was involved in a company program, and it was great. The first mentor I had was wonderful, but she left the company before we got going. The company then assigned me to someone else, but he isn't so hot. Now what do I do?" We also hear, "Oh mentoring—there's a program at my company, but I'm not involved in it."

Regardless of whether you are involved in a corporate mentoring program or have decided to create your own personal mentoring agenda, there are pros and cons to each. Research suggests that "planned marriages"—meaning relationships that are created by someone else—are not as good as those that form through "natural selection." The latter is where you both come together spontaneously because there is good chemistry. A planned marriage might have good chemistry, but that probably is the exception rather than the rule. A corporate program may have a proven structure, and structured relationships have a tendency to be successful. However, a personal mentoring relationship using natural selection, in which you have a self-imposed structure as well as good chemistry, will typically be more successful than a corporate arrangement where you are matched with someone else.

In either situation, the bottom line is *you only get out of the mentoring relationship what you put into it.* One of the biggest benefits of a planned marriage arrangement is you don't have to go through all the steps of prequalification—you already have a person who is ready, willing, and able to get started. Having such a program available at your job provides a unique opportunity, and you should certainly take advantage of it. Learn what you can from it, and use it as an example of what you want or don't want from your next mentoring relationship.

We often remind people with concerns about their corporate mentors that they need more than one mentor. Certain people are happy with only one, but our experience has been that it is far more effective to have several. Even if your company has provided you with a mentor, that person is probably your company or industry mentor only—he or she is not going to be able to meet all your needs as your career progresses, nor be likely to fulfill that role indefinitely. In a given field, you may have two or three mentors, or you could have one mentor in that area and four more mentors in four different areas. Just because you have been in a mentoring relationship previously or currently have a mentor doesn't mean you shouldn't go out and get another one. If you have a bad experience in a corporate mentoring program, it doesn't mean all future experiences will be unsatisfactory.

If you do get paired at work with someone you don't like, remember this: *everyone* has some pearl of wisdom to offer. This harkens back to Dale Carnegie's lesson of how to win friends and influence people. Be nice to people and they usually will like you. If you feel negative toward your assigned mentor, he or she probably will be able to tell, and the relationship will have trouble—meaning you will have trouble. Ask yourself why you think the match was made and look for a deeper meaning in the relationship. If you have the opportunity to be partnered with someone in a structured program, try to go into it with an open mind and learn from it what you can. Not everyone is going to be an amazing, magical mentor, but all have something to contribute, if you search deep enough.

4. What Is Required of a Mentor and Protégé in Terms of Time and Resources?

As a mentor, you should be willing to put enough into the relationship to be successful, but success depends upon your expectations. Traditionally, what is required depends on the depth of the partnership. The more involved you are, the more that is required of you. If both of you want a casual arrangement where you meet occasionally for a little coaching, then it probably isn't going to take much. As a protégé, it isn't going to cost you more than a phone call and a lunch or two. As a mentor, you are looking at a few limited consultation periods and must be willing to be interrupted when you probably are involved in something else.

On the other hand, if the mentor is willing to commit to mutually agreed upon goals with the protégé—as are a few mentors we know, who map out specific agendas and give their protégés tasks to accomplish—then the program is going to be more involved. The protégé, for instance, will have to invest more time to accomplish his task list. Sometimes that might mean a protégé will have to spend time training. Some mentors act only as sounding boards off of whom protégés bounce their ideas, others serve as trainers and actually walk protégés through the entire process. It depends on the depth of the relationship, the mentor's experience, and what the partners committed to at the outset.

A mentor's time usually is spent with the protégé reviewing a project, discussing an option, or giving direction. These meetings, even if only on the telephone, can impose upon one's personal life and sometimes will interfere with one's work. In the initial stages of the relationship, the mentor almost universally is giving more than he or she is getting in return. However, that is by no means time wasted. As the protégé evolves, the mentor slowly comes to see the payoff from his or her investment.

Your commitment in time as a protégé can be quite significant. If you have a mentor who assigns specific tasks to perform, you may not be prepared or may not know how much time it will take to do the things on your list. The legwork—research, telephoning, or interviewing people—can be quite time consuming. The protégé may be surprised at the amount of work the mentor assigns. If you find the pace too hard to keep up with, you might discuss with your mentor your long-term goals to see if you are in line. For instance you could say, "This is how much time I have. This is my five-year plan (three-year plan, two-year plan, etc.), and I want to set a course based on my goals for this time frame."

Since time is money, every minute that a mentor spends with a protégé costs him or his company money. For the protégé, however, every pearl of wisdom picked up from the mentor is going to save time, which also translates into money at some future point. There is rarely an exchange of money between the mentor and the protégé for services; however, this is not unheard of. For example, a creative solution for providing a more immediate benefit to the mentor is found in the Mentoring Systems, Inc. insurance sales program. The protégé—who is a new sales professional—has to set up all the appointments. The mentor—a senior sales professional—has to go with the protégé on the sales calls. For the first six months, they split the commissions down the middle.

The mentor's incentive, therefore, is that she doesn't have to set up the appointments, all she has to do is show up. She doesn't have to do all the leg work, but she gets half the commission. The protégé's incentive is knowing that whatever appointments are made, there is a much higher chance of closing the sale now with the help of the mentor than there would be if he were on his own. The protégé benefits from the mentor's experience and receives half of whatever the mentor is able to close. There is a give-and-take involving money, and relationships can work effectively this way. If you want a top producer to mentor you and he is concerned about what he will get out of it, you might propose a similar arrangement. You split the commission with him if he goes on the appointment you set. This way, you can watch him and learn how he closes a sale. This option has been done in some organizations, especially in a selling environment.

As far as the cost of resources, requirements are usually determined by the expectations of the mentor as well as the depth of the relationship. While the mentor might lend the protégé reading or training materials or allow him to work on his computer, it is difficult to put an actual dollar value on "costs." In any case, the value derived will, we believe, far exceed any costs incurred.

5. When Is It Time to End the Mentor/Protégé Relationship?

If the mentor/protégé relationship begins to sour, remember that such a union is not meant to last forever. Mentors are part of a life transition for you, and you are part of a life transition for them. You may not remain at that transition point for an extended period. Most often, the mentor serves as a guide to help the protégé get to a new level of accomplishment. All things end sooner or later, or at least they evolve into new beginnings. It is time for a protégé to leave if the relationship is not empowering. If you don't feel inspired and excited from the interaction, it's a good sign things could be winding down.

The other determining factor of whether to continue is the measure of productivity of the relationship. For instance, you might spend time together, but suddenly you realize, "This is nice and I'm having a wonderful time, but it's not productive!" Essentially what you have then is a social, not a mentoring, relationship. In these situations, it might be time to find someone new.

Another factor that might lead to a breakup is if you simply don't respect the mentor's advice anymore. The following story by Michael Jeffreys, professional speaker and author, illustrates his dilemma about how to handle a close mentor who developed another compelling interest.

THE WIZARD'S APPRENTICE

My first mentor came into my life when I was just beginning in magic. I was 14 years old and had recently started a magic club at my junior high school. One day, a professional magician came to our school to put on a magic show during assembly. His name was Josh, and he called himself "The Wizard of Westminster." I laughed and marveled with the rest of the kids in the audience that day, and thought, "Now that's what I want to be when I grow up, a real magician!"

After the show, I got the surprise of my life when my art teacher told me that the magician wanted to meet the president of the

continues

continued

school's magic club. "Me?" I stammered excitedly. "He wants to meet me?" I couldn't believe my luck. I ran to my locker to get the portrait of Houdini that I had been working on so I could show him. When I returned to class, there he was!

He was in his mid-twenties, had blond hair, wore a black velvet cape trimmed in emerald green with a large ruby broach pinned to it, a white ruffled tuxedo shirt, a big black velvet bow-tie, black slacks, and shiny black dress shoes. In his right hand was a top hat with a live rabbit named Alexander III! When my teacher introduced us, he smiled at me and then reached down and pulled a cigarette from behind my ear as he asked, "Aren't you a little young to be smoking?" My friends and I all giggled. Next, he lit the cigarette, took a puff, and made it disappear right before our eyes! Forget Superman, I had found my hero!

I showed him my poster of Houdini, and he seemed impressed. After doing a few more tricks, he asked me if I'd like to come over to his house and see some of his bigger illusions. I was thrilled. After school the next day, I took the bus to his house. When he invited me in, I couldn't believe my eyes. It looked like a magic factory! There were big tricks, small tricks, shelves filled with magic books, and Merlin statues and twinkling lights all over the place. I thought I had died and gone to magic heaven.

By the end of the evening we had established a bond. It was at that point that he asked me if I wanted to be his apprentice. "Wow, the wizard's apprentice! How cool," I thought and, of course, said yes immediately. Soon, I was accompanying him to his magic shows at big department stores like Bullocks and Robinsons.

The stores would have these events called "Breakfast with the Easter Bunny" and "Breakfast with Santa Claus," and Josh would be hired to do a magic show for the couple of hundred of kids that would show up with their parents for breakfast. It was a great experience for me as I would help him set up his tricks, assist him during the performance, and then pack up the illusions afterwards. On the drive home we would always discuss the show, what worked, what didn't, and why.

During the six years we were together we became very close, shared hundreds of adventures and humorous experiences, and through it all I learned a lot. However, while I wish I could say everything went smoothly, sadly, it didn't. As it turned out, the man

continues

concluded

I looked up to—who had been like a big brother to me—had gotten into drugs, first using them, and later selling them.

When we first met, I was at the bottom of the ladder and he was near the top. Now, six years later, we had switched places. I was now working restaurants and getting lucrative magic jobs, and he had lost his motivation and drive. While I wanted to rehearse and work on improving ourselves and creating new magic, he wanted to spend his time doing other things, most of which were illegal. Soon, paranoia set in and when people with guns began showing up looking for him, I knew it was time to permanently sever our relationship.

However, something good did come of it all. As a result of my experience, I created a drug awareness program called, "Magic Is Fun. Drugs are Dumb!," which I have been performing at schools throughout Southern California for the past 10 years. Every time I step in front of an auditorium full of 300–400 kids, I always try to give them the same sense of wonder and entertainment that Josh had given me and the other kids at my school two decades earlier.

My mentor taught me many wonderful things, and for that I'll always be grateful, but he also taught me a few things I knew I didn't want to emulate. Sometimes, part of the responsibility of having a mentor is knowing when you have outgrown each other and realizing when it's time to move on.

You might also wonder, when is the time for the *mentor* to end things? If you invest a lot of time with a protégé who is not following through on the assignments you give or isn't taking action on the ideas you pass along, eventually you will begin to feel you're wasting your time. *"Why am I sitting here telling this person all this and trying to help him when he doesn't do anything with what I'm giving him?"* If you start to feel this way, it's time either to end the relationship or at least set a few limits. "I've given you these 16 things to do, and I don't want to meet with you again until you have accomplished them. I feel I'm being repetitive, and I'm not enjoying that."

The other thing for you as a mentor to remember is that if you start to feel competitive with your protégé and notice you are steering her in the direction of *your* best interests—not *her* best interests—you should take a long look in the mirror. Your duty as a mentor is to avoid obstructing the path of your protégé. Your job is to empower this person to be the best at whatever it is that she is trying to become. If things get too competitive, you might consider ending the relationship, or at least letting it evolve into a more relaxed relationship than that of mentor and protégé.

Sometimes a relationship dissolves because of obstacles beyond the control of either party. It should not be taken personally. Be thankful that you had the experience. We always try to keep connected with past friends, even if it means only sending them an annual Christmas card. If you are a protégé, and the mentor has obligations or responsibilities that cause him or her to push you away, you need to be ready for that possibility and accept it when it comes. Neither is there any reason to be resentful. Be thankful for the pearls of wisdom you received during your time together. We always try to leave every relationship on a happy and positive note, thankful for the time we spent together and for the information our mentors shared with us. The mentor is not obligated to us for life. Nor are you obligated to be a protégé for life. You are obligated, however, to be respectful of each another and to recognize each other for the time you spent together.

6. There Are Very Few Women in My Industry, and Even Fewer Who Want to Be Mentors—What Should I Do?

Women may find it somewhat difficult to locate a willing female mentor. The problem is that experienced women traditionally are more reluctant to serve as mentors than their male counterparts. As a result, the woman who wants to advance her career through the help of a mentor faces some difficulties doing so. In many industries, there are fewer women than men in management positions to serve as mentors. In others, such as health care, mentoring activities in general actually dropped off as women ascended into the ranks of management because men didn't want the problems that after-hours mixed gender relationships could create.

Even when experienced women are available as mentors, in a corporate setting they sometimes are less willing than men to serve as mentors. Studies indicate that many women in management believe they have had to try so hard to get where they are that they simply don't have time to mentor anyone. The fact few women want to become mentors causes a problem for young women who would prefer a female mentor. As an increasing number of women move into management roles there should be more opportunities for midcareer females to mentor less experienced women. Timing plays a part in whether someone will, or can, serve as a mentor. It often depends upon the stresses placed on a woman by her career and family. Hopefully more women will choose to become mentors since doing so offers a host of potential benefits, not only to protégés, but also to them. These include rejuvenation of their careers, recognition from their organizations, improved job performance, and a loyal base of support.

In citing reasons why more women don't serve as mentors, researchers say women are particularly sensitive to the overall risks of mentoring. You incur increased visibility after becoming someone's mentor, and it reflects on you if your protégé fails. Sometimes people fear a mentoring relationship because they don't want to incur that risk. We don't think that is necessarily a gender issue, but studies have suggested that women who lack experience may be sensitive to this issue, perhaps more so than men. If this is a reason why some women choose not to be mentors, then we need to be aware of it and work toward creating environments where they don't feel threatened by the risk of a protégé's indiscretions.

Meanwhile, if you are a woman having difficulty finding a female mentor, you may have to consider the next best thing—a man. Although it may be more difficult to find a female mentor than a male, that doesn't mean that you should forego establishing a mentoring relationship. A mentor is particularly important for a woman who faces organizational barriers to advancement.

If you are in a situation where you might prefer a woman but none is open to the suggestion, then search for a male mentor. Although the majority of Terri's mentors have been male, that doesn't mean she wouldn't like a female mentor. Three of the four protégés she is now mentoring are men; one is a woman.

Sometimes a man will feel uncomfortable mentoring a woman because there are gender issues that may reflect negatively on him. In our seminars, we hear comments from men such as, "I met this young woman—she was great, and I was mentoring her, but there was a reaction. People said, 'Oh she must be sleeping with him since he's always helping her out.' What do I do in that situation?"

This is a sensitive area, no doubt, for everyone involved. Our only advice is to simply do the right thing. By that we mean ignore narrow-minded gossipmongers who would stunt a young woman's career growth in the name of "propriety."

While not wanting to overreact to unfair criticism, it helps to formalize your relationship and set strict limits on where it is going from the beginning. It should be clear from the start this is neither a social nor a romantic endeavor. The male mentor must clarify that to a starry-eyed female protégé just as surely as the female protégé must outline it for an inappropriately enthusiastic male mentor. If you can't distance yourself from the other person, then you should-n't attempt a serious mentoring relationship. The point here is to beat the system—not fall victim to it.

What can you do if people start slandering you? Hold your head high and consider the source. We need merely to acknowledge that these issues are present and would like to encourage readers, particularly young women, to reach for the best that they can be, regardless of the jealousy they may inspire as they move up the lad-der of success. Maintain a code of ethics, stick to your principles, and be true to yourself. Don't let other peoples' opinions affect your efforts to learn the ropes. If you always conduct yourself in a man-ner that displays class and shows people what your relationship with your mentor or protégé really is—friendship based on coach-ing—then that is all anyone is ever going to see. Carry yourself with dignity and always reinforce the fact that you are only friends. Your language should suggest that this person is your mentor and you are his protégé. If people get a different impression, tell them they are misinformed. It only reflects their limited outlook. Remember, you never want to give people a reason to think otherwise.

As a mentor, it helps to establish other relationships so that it doesn't appear as though you are playing favorites. Broaden your interests so you are helping several people who also are trying to accomplish worthwhile goals. This will tend to deflect potential criticism. Set guidelines for meetings and get-togethers with your protégés that are socially correct—luncheon rather than dinner meetings, discussions in public places or business offices rather than hotel rooms or your personal residences. A few precautions such as these will help you to further the hopes of a young person with a promising career and not risk either of your reputations.

STEPPING OVER THE LINE

When one of our colleagues first started spending time with her mentor at work, their relationship was strictly business. He was her supervisor at that point. He later switched companies, but they still stayed in touch with each other. Since they weren't working together any longer, several comments began to creep into the conversation that suggested he was interested in dating her.

The first couple of remarks she ignored. She justified them by saying the two of them were enjoying a more relaxed relationship now that they were no longer working together. When she realized that he definitely was interested in a romantic relationship, she was certain she didn't want that to happen. Her response: "Bill, I really like you, I respect you, and I admire the work that you have done. I've always held you in the highest regard. You are my mentor. But I am not interested in any form of a relationship with you other than that. I'm concerned now that you're telling me this is going to affect our mentoring relationship." They talked about it, and he said he heard her "loud and clear." He never brought it up again, and it became a nonissue.

That type of direct response may be the best that is possible given the situation. A woman must remember that at any point she becomes uncomfortable, the best thing to do is to end the relationship. If she tries talking about it with her mentor and it doesn't work, then she should sever the connection.

7. Have People Ever Insinuated the Authors' Relationship Was More Than Simply Mentor and Protégé?

Sometimes people have drawn inferences from our relationship and wondered out loud whether anything is going on. Both of us are concerned about this because Floyd dearly loves his wife and is totally committed to her. There never has been and never will be anything romantic between us. Though we are close and can speak openly on most subjects, we are cautious about never doing anything that would make anybody question our principles and sincerity. It is important not only to behave appropriately but also to *appear* to behave appropriately because of the feelings of the other people in our lives, be they boyfriend or wife. We are not going to restrict our professional relationship because of the unfounded suspicions of a few shallow people, but neither are we going to ignore the potential for pain that a false accusation could cause to us or to the loved ones around us on whom we depend for support.

Personally, we try to be gender blind when we think about mentoring relationships. We gather pearls of wisdom from as many people as we possibly can and don't make gender an issue. We try to eliminate it from the equation entirely because mentoring is not about gender—it's about knowledge. Teachers come in all races, colors, sizes, creeds, and experience levels. Therefore, you should try to be gender and color blind.

8. What Is the Best Possible Outcome of Your Mentoring Relationship?

Once you have been working with your mentor for awhile you begin to wonder if you will ever learn everything they have to teach you. The pearls of wisdom will gradually emerge from your mentor over time. You will earn the right to hear increasingly secret and important pearls of wisdom as you progress along the road your mentor has mapped out for you. We believe you will never stop learning from some mentors. These highly accomplished individuals know when you are ready to hear more and deliver it to you only when you are ready for it. To get to the stage where you have learned everything this person has to teach means you know as much about the subject as they do. While that is perhaps possible, the chances are remote, particularly if your mentor has been involved in this field for many years.

The usual approach of learning what you can from a mentor and then moving on to someone else is normal and acceptable. However, in our view, the best possible outcome for a protégé who wants to continue his or her relationship with a mentor is for the protégé to eventually give something truly significant back to the mentor. As the relationship begins, the mentor coaches the protégé as he moves forward with his career or personal quest for knowledge and accomplishment. The protégé will grow in a unique way because not only is he influenced by the mentor, but he also is exposed to many other life experiences that are going on at the same time as the mentor's coaching. So the protégé develops new and unique skills and knowledge that the mentor may not possess.

Since the objective of mentoring is to coach the protégé into becoming more capable and independent, it is a natural step for the protégé to evolve into someone who can operate effectively without a mentor. However, another choice is also available. We will assume that the mentor has invested a lot of time in the growth of the protégé, and that there is an unpaid debt to the mentor. One way to repay it is by passing the experience on to another protégé. However, it also can be repaid by giving something directly back to the mentor.

Let's consider the value to the mentor of the protégé's newly acquired assets. The mentor presumably saw something in the protégé to persuade her to become his mentor. The protégé likely had raw talent and a sincere interest in learning. With added experiences now, the protégé can undertake important projects that would enhance the mentor's standing. If the protégé is gaining insight and skills from the mentor, he is moving toward an eventual parity with the mentor. What better way to recognize that accomplishment and repay the mentor for her time and teachings than for the protégé and mentor to come together and create something that neither could make on his or her own?

In our view, this is the best possible long-term outcome of a mentoring relationship. For the protégé and mentor to someday have the opportunity to create something together that neither could alone symbolizes the accomplishments of both individuals and recognizes the positive outcome of their time together.

We have listed a few of the most common questions regarding the mentor/protégé relationship, but we know there are more than those we have cited. While not all these issues are likely to surface in your mentor/protégé relationships, it is nevertheless worthwhile to have some background in areas that others have found obstacles. Be open to the realization that, as with all human relations, good mentor/protégé associations continue to grow based on both people bringing new information, experiences, and vitality to the union. The key to this longevity is having a commitment, being open with your communication, and expressing a willingness to negotiate.

We should also emphasize that good mentor/protégé relations are supported by the understanding that a mentor has a limited responsibility. The mentor is not the protégé's personal teacher. A teacher is different from a mentor. Teaching may be a part of mentoring, but a mentor holds a very special place in the life of a protégé. The relationship is unique. The focus of this book is on showing how mentoring is "the final secret" to success, when you have taken all the available training, read all the books, and are now asking, what's next? That something—that final secret of putting it all together—involves serving under a mentor or mentoring someone less experienced than yourself.

We will next take a look at some special types of mentors, including momentary mentors, and the role that parents and grandparents can play in the mentoring lifestyle.

HIGHLIGHTS

- ❖ There always will be challenges in a mentor/protégé or any other kind of human relationship.
- ❖ Finding a suitable mentor may require a significant amount of personal initiative.
- ❖ Openness between the mentor and the protégé can eliminate problems and holds the only possibility for saving a relationship that is imbalanced in terms of commitment.
- ❖ Mentors can expect to give more to the protégé than they receive in return.
- ❖ Most mentor/protégé relationships end sooner or later— it's just a question of when.
- ❖ Women who would prefer a female mentor, but can't find one, may have to "settle" for a man.
- ❖ Completing a joint project may be the culmination of a mentor/protégé relationship.

CHAPTER

The Magic of Mentoring

Whose permission are you seeking that will allow you to go for it? Ken Wallace

In the last chapter we went over common difficulties encountered while trying to adopt a mentoring lifestyle and find a suitable mentor or protégé. Armed with those suggestions and the 16 Laws of Mentoring, you should now be well prepared to start your search for a mentor or protégé. Remember, we recommend that everyone *have both* and *be both*. While traditionally a person is a protégé first, then moves on to become a mentor later, we believe the true mentoring lifestyle ordains that you be a protégé to one person and a mentor to another *at the same time*. However, finding a mentor may be more challenging than finding a protégé, since the mentor is generally the one who makes the largest investment in the relationship. A good place to start easily is at home: Parents, grandparents, and other relatives are probably your *original* mentors.

FAMILY AS MENTORS

Sometimes, when we are searching for a sign of good fortune, we overlook the four-leaf clover directly beneath our feet. If you want to find a four-leaf clover, you have to bend down and look for one. If you want to win the lottery, you have to play. In your immediate realm of friends, family, and acquaintances, there may be someone you already know—perhaps even someone you live with—who understands what it takes to be successful. Remember, we don't define success as being wealthy. In our view, success is being happy. If you are not content with your life and your accomplishments, then you can't convince us you are successful, even if you are rich. Conversely, just because you may not be wealthy doesn't mean you aren't successful. If you have lived your life on your own terms and accomplished your dream—whether it be to raise a family or start a business—then you have a legacy to pass on to the next generation.

Our first mentors are usually our parents, and sometimes they are the best ones we ever have. Sometimes we put them in a different category, however, and we don't learn everything from them that we could. Because they are family, we don't take full advantage of all the knowledge they possess.

Terri has recently been exploring the experiences her relatives had during their earlier years. Without actually asking these people, you very often never really get the full picture and all the interesting stories they have to tell. She learned, for instance, about the heroic efforts her grandmother made during World War II to fly overseas and rescue her sister and children after her brother-in-law suddenly died. And Terri's grandfather gave her a lesson in perseverance when she probed about his experiences in Europe during the same war as bombers were delivering terror from overhead.

Many times our closest and most trusted mentors are family members. People have shared many amazing stories with us. Below are several about mentors who made a difference in the lives of people around them that might help you as you implement your personal mentoring plan. They inspired either their family or friends to keep working, to keep searching for a better reality.

Herb Lloyd of Service Sales Consultants Seminars, Inc., of Orem, Utah, submitted the following narrative about his father.

A LESSON IN EXCELLENCE

My mentor walked a proud, fast pace that was hard to keep up with. My father had only an eighth-grade education, but taught me more about people and selling than anyone else in my life—and I have hundreds of tapes from some of the greatest salesmen alive. My dad

continues

concluded

bought and sold livestock, and, as a youth, I spent many hours on the road with him. One way he would get a chuckle from prospects, who regularly chided, "How does someone who looks like you have such beautiful daughters?," was by saying: "The bigger and uglier the buck, the better looking the lambs." Needless to say, he was down to earth.

One of Dad's stories in particular had a big impact on my life. Dad was in the school band, and there was a drummer named Bicksley. This fellow played the bass drum so timidly you could barely hear it. He tried to muffle it out of fear of making a mistake. One day the band leader yelled at him out of frustration, "Damn it, Bicksley, beat that drum! If you make a mistake—make a big one."

Even as an adult, whenever I consider a new direction or am worried about leaving my comfort zone, I remember that story. It has given me the courage to overcome doubt, fear, and opposition from others. It has let me soar to remarkable heights.

I could go on regarding Dad's thoughts about honor, honesty, and integrity—a man's word is his bond, and so forth—but his last years really typified his feelings about excellence .

At 62, Dad suffered a heart attack. Doctors told him that if he stayed home, went on a diet, and modified his life he could live to a ripe old age. He looked the doctor in the eye and said, "That's not living for me."

He subsequently took a job as the custodian of our church. Many view custodial work as menial, but not Dad. The church became his pride and joy. After he started, you could see your face in the hall tiles, they glistened so. People commented about his helpful attitude, the cleanliness of the church, his smile, and his jovial spirit.

It was while he was on duty at the church that he died. Though it's been 30 years since he passed away, there's not a day that goes by that I don't think of him, his life, his love of people, and dedication to service.

Someone who knew my father once honored me as no one else ever has.

"You remind me of your dad," he said.

I couldn't have asked for a nicer compliment.

Parents make great mentors, even if sometimes we wish they would follow the 16 Laws!

The truth is they always are available for advice (sometimes when we don't even know we need it), and parents represent a valuable resource to the protégé on a quest for information and in search of the valued but elusive pearls of wisdom. Words and phrases that our parents use when we are five years old somehow come back to mind again when we are 50 as we search for a way to overcome what seems like the most difficult problem we ever faced. Those who have the good fortune of having parents or grandparents who still are alive should take the time to listen for their pearls of wisdom. There may be valuable lessons you overlooked as you became obsessed with the requirements of earning a living and raising your own family.

Ken Wallace wanted to change careers, but he wasn't sure it was the right thing to do. He knew his father would tell him honestly if he thought it wasn't a good idea.

THE POWER TO GO FOR IT

There is power in language to create an inner reality, which then translates into behavior to make our internal reality externally real. The last conversation I had with my father was about my desire to become a professional speaker, trainer, and consultant. I told him I didn't know much about the profession or even what topics I would address, but I felt strongly that I should pursue it.

After I had finished, the clear hazel eyes of this gentle man gazed into my expectant expression and, after a few moments of thoughtful silence, my father said, "Go for it!" The next day he died suddenly.

Every time I encounter an obstacle that would prevent me from doing what I know I can, I gain strength from that final conversation I had with Dad. Overcoming obstacles is not as difficult as it once was.

Among the many words of wisdom expressed by Ralph Waldo Emerson, some of the most powerful are, "Our chief want in life is for someone to make us do what we can."

My father encouraged me to do what we both believed I could do by giving me his permission. He pulled the trigger on the starting gun.

You and I possess the power of language to encourage other people's beliefs in their own abilities and dreams. Through language we have the power to give others a passion for what they can do with their lives. We also have the power, even the responsibility, to empower them to do what they know they can.

continues

concluded

What is it that you can do with your life? What is it that you are not doing but that you know you can do? Whose permission are you seeking that will allow you to "go for it?"

The following warm and charming letters are from two high school students who wrote to us about the warm feelings they have toward their parents, the most important mentors they have known up to this point in their lives.

HAVING A FRIEND FOR LIFE

Dear Dad,

I want to thank you for teaching me real-world responsibility. I learned a lot from you on how to be a man.

When I think back to the times when we fought, I think of how immature I was and how right you were about many things. Whenever I made a mistake, you took time out to help me with it. No matter what you were doing, you always put me first. I would do things wrong, and you always corrected me in a positive way.

You taught me how to fiddle with things and make them work again. When I needed help with my homework, I'd run to you for assistance. If I slacked off, you were always there to tell me to work my best. I remember how hard I tried to be like you because you were such a great father.

In the seventh grade, I needed to do a project, and nobody would help me but my dad—he made the time because he loved me. I was very proud to have a dad like you. Back when I was on the football team, you came to every game just to show me your support. We also had fun when you showed me how to play golf, tennis, and baseball. I remember when I played baseball, I hated how you coached me when I played on your team. But now that I am older and look back on it, it showed me how much you cared because you gave me all of that time. My mentor was a friend for life. I miss you very much dad.

Brian Sullivan
Fullerton High School
Fullerton, Calif.

continues

GETTING A LITTLE PUSH

When I was young, I was very timid and shy. I was afraid to talk to strangers, and I would rather die than speak in public. I admired people who could make such eloquent speeches in front of crowds. All the eyes would stare at them, and they would not even flinch! It was my only wish to be like one of them. But I could never do that, I told myself several times.

I could remember just one occasion that ultimately changed my view. It was the tenth winter of my life. The church that I attended for five years held a Bible speech contest every winter. Only students who were extremely brave could recite or tell a story from the Bible in front of all the church members. I have always been one of the crowd, even though my dream was to be up on stage making a speech.

That winter, my Sunday school teacher asked me if I would be interested in trying out for the contest. Of course I was thrilled, but my mouth said the usual, "No." I desperately wanted to do it, but I was really frightened. I did not know what scared me so much that I could give up things that I would love to try. When my mom heard about my refusal, she told me something that I would never forget. "It does not matter how well or how poorly you can do something," she said. "What matters is that you will always wonder and regret why you did not try. It is important to have a passion for things you love."

I was too young to understand what she meant exactly. But it gave me a sense of push and encouragement. I would not want to spend the rest of my life just wondering what I could have done. I certainly would like to look back later and not regret my choices. So I signed up for that speech contest after all. And to everyone's surprise, including mine, I won first place!

But winning did not seem important. The most important thing was the "push" that my mom had placed in my heart—permanently.

Seven years have passed since then, and I have won numerous debate and speech awards. Now my favorite hobby is to make speeches and meet new people. Whenever I see my mom in the audience among the big crowd while I am on stage, I still remember that day when I first decided to sign up and speak in public. And I always feel the warm tears of sincere gratitude. My mom believed in me and supported my trying new things when I doubted my ability. When I failed, she never forgot to remind me of the "push."

continues

---

concluded

Sometimes I still feel afraid to do something new. Then I remind myself of her little bit of wisdom that will always give me the push I need.

My mom has been the best mentor and support I have ever had, and ever will have. Thank you, Mom.

Jennie S. Park
Sunny Hills High School
Buena Park, California

MOMENTARY MENTORS

Our lives are made up of a series of experiences that, when sewn together, produce a patchwork quilt, an historical record of all we ever saw and heard, all we thought, and everything we did. During the course of these experiences certain things that people say stand out in our minds as being particularly relevant. In fact, most people secretly are on the lookout for these pearls of wisdom, buoys that provide markers as we chug our way through the fog of life, never knowing for certain what is around the next jetty. People will come into our lives for a year, a day, or maybe only an hour yet they will leave us enriched with an increased knowledge of life, a perception that is summed up in just a few words. Though we may never see them again, their message stays with us forever. We call these people *momentary mentors.*

One of our friends, Jason, has a gift with animals. You might find him out on the beach in the morning feeding the seagulls dried bread. His antidote for depression is to go to a pet store and play with the puppies. "It is impossible to feel discouraged when you have a puppy to play with," he would say. The interesting thing about his unconventional remedy for tough times is that it seems to work, not only for him but for others. When a particularly moving song would play on the radio, Jason would frequently stop whatever he was doing, listen, and think about what is going on around him. His pearl of wisdom is: *be aware of and enjoy the moment in which you are living.*

Larne Neuland, a colleague in South Africa, writes how her outlook was changed by an old man whose gift was showing her how to be grateful for what life gives, not resentful for what it denies.

AN OLD-TIMER'S POSITIVE OUTLOOK

I am a native of beautiful South Africa, and my hometown was Somerset West, situated in the Cape Province—the southernmost portion of the African continent. A jewel of a village, it is located in the heart of the Hottentots Holland mountain range, and five minutes away a naked coastline exposes pearly turquoise charm. It's a great little place.

It was there that a remarkable old man left me with a priceless gift, without ever being aware of it. Jim, as he is fondly known, is a familiar figure in the little town. He wears a moth-eaten yet brightly colored red cap and also sports a scraggy beard. Looks moth-eaten too. Blind in one eye, he can usually be found sitting on the wall next to the library, reading a newspaper with his one good eye. Crippled by a charging bull when he was a young man, Ol' Jim cannot walk without the aid of a steel cane. More than a block away, you can hear him coming down the road as his cane connects with tarmac.

Although he's an old man, Jim enjoys working, and one of his permanent jobs was being my gardener. I use the term "gardener" with some trepidation because what he did in my garden was not customary gardening. He worked for me on Monday mornings and would rake together all the scattered leaves in the area. This leaf pile would always be strategically positioned in full view of my office window. The old man would never put the leaves in a garbage bag. Although he had the use of only one eye, he was not in the least short-sighted. At his advanced age, one has to plan ahead and think of the future! Fortunately, Somerset West is a windy town, and the following Monday, the leaves would be joyful chaos. Ol' Jim was still in business.

I didn't pay him very much money. When he first applied for the position, I told him I couldn't afford a gardener at this stage of my career. He insisted on working for whatever I could pay him, and a cup of hot coffee and a sandwich would suffice if things were "really tight," he added with a ghost of a smile. However, regardless of the amount he received each week, Jim did not spare the money a second glance before pocketing it.

"Hah! Give a man a cup of coffee and some bread," he would chuckle.

continues

concluded

Jim used my house as a kind of stopover on his way home, a few times each week. The cane would be heard, eventually followed by crusty baritones.

"Coffee and bread! A man needs to warm his innards!"

Either I or one of the children would fill a mug with hot coffee, cut two thick slices of bread, slap on some jam, and hand the rough meal to the old man. The unappealing truth of the matter is that the bread I used for Jim's sandwiches was not always fresh, very often my leftovers. The jam might be a flavor that the children didn't enjoy or the runny homemade calamity. But Ol' Jim wouldn't mind, he wasn't fussy. One had to bear in mind that times were not easy, and I had mouths to feed. And Jim came around so *often*. My excellent reasoning quieted the pestering guilt which ate at my conscience.

One day Ol' Jim's voice bellowed from the kitchen door.

"Excuse me, Ma'am. I want to talk to Ma'am about the sandwiches."

The sandwiches! My heart skipped a beat. Attack being the only defense I knew, I marched to the door and stared the old man squarely in his one eye.

"And *what about* the sandwiches, Jim?"

That's when he gave me the priceless gift—the one I will always treasure.

"Ma'am," said Jim. "I want to tell you that your sandwiches are the most delicious I have ever tasted. Ma'am—you always put some jam on them, and they taste so good!"

To many, Ol' Jim may appear to have nothing at all. To me, he has everything. He has the princely treasure that many spend their lives searching for and few ever attain. Life always sparkles for Ol' Jim. That's because *when the bread is stale, he tastes the jam.*

I will never forget the living example demonstrated so clearly to me. Every time life seems unfair and the going gets tough, every time life hands me a blow and my plans are shattered, I forget about the stale bread and look for the jam.

As we close the final chapter, let's take a moment to reflect on all the material we have covered. We hope we have presented sufficient evidence to convince you that mentoring works and have explained why it is so effective. We have given you several approaches to finding a mentor and have compiled a detailed list of guidelines so that your mentoring relationships can succeed; the rest is up to you. You have to weigh whether reaching your goal is worth the effort for you to go out there and find someone who is going to show you exactly how it's done. Remember, a mentor will spend the necessary time with you—free of charge—to show you exactly what it takes because you have convinced him or her that you have the right stuff to succeed. You have impressed him that you can be as good as he is, that you can be *like him*. He will do it because it means his ideas and knowledge will be passed along to someone worthy of receiving that guarded and precious information.

This will be someone you trust, someone who knows what he or she is talking about. You know that he has learned the secrets to the success you are so hungry to achieve because you have carefully reviewed his background and found he already has done it. He has proven himself in real-life tests of wits and perseverance. You may be in a fog about what to do next, but he has already done it and then gone on to something else. He is ahead of you and you need him to tell you how to proceed in this maze that threatens to kill your spirit, dampen your appetite, and force you to give up and go home, a late entry in life's book of near successes. Don't do it! There is hope, and the hope comes from learning where to get critical inside information about what you want, what you are willing to work and fight for, information on how to achieve the most important thing in your life: *your personal dream*.

We wish you great happiness and success on your journey, and in closing we want to leave you with several truisms to consider as you begin your own search for knowledge. Following is a collection of pearls of wisdom from individuals who were generous enough to share with us what it took them a lifetime to learn.

HIGHLIGHTS

- ❖ Parents and family members can many times serve as the greatest mentors ever.
- ❖ We must remember to be open to and aware of the momentary mentors who leave us with an enriched perspective on life even though our time with them may be very brief.

❖ The mentoring process provides a road map for success to accomplishing your personal dreams.

❖ The key to obtaining your dreams is to remember that mentoring relationships aid you on your journey—they are not your destination.

Pearls of Wisdom: Mentoring at Work

Following are words of wisdom from the mentors of a number of well-known and successful protégés.

Zig Ziglar
Author/Motivational Teacher
Mentor: Fred Smith

My mentor, Fred Smith, taught me that all good students are not necessarily good thinkers. They frequently continue in the pursuit of knowledge and information without taking quiet time to think creatively on how they can use that information.

For example, when I'm walking, I never listen to tapes of any kind but use that time to prayerfully explore how I can use the knowledge I have in a more effective way.

Jim Rohn
Author/Speaker/Trainer
Mentor: Earl Shoaff

Work harder on myself than I do on my job. Working hard on your job will make you a living; working hard on yourself will make you a fortune!

I was always a hard worker on my job, and, of course, I continued to be one. But I started working on myself—reading books, attending seminars, and getting around other successful people. I worked on my language, my handshake, my health, and my finances. That's when my whole life turned around.

Kyle Wilson
President, Jim Rohn International
Mentor: Jim Rohn

Jim Rohn told me in my early years as a promoter that the greatest wealth I would find would not be directly from selling seminar tickets, but from the future associations I would encounter.

Seven years later, I have found that by serving and bringing value to the marketplace, overwhelmingly the relationships with others that I've formed have paid the greatest financial and personal returns back to me.

Christopher Atkins
Mentor: Jerry Mintz

When all else fails, help someone else. Many times I have applied this pearl of wisdom, whether within my own home or with others, and each time I am filled with a sense of well-being. There was one time in particular that I carry with me and think about often. I was in a place of tremendous fear and emotional pain. Jerry told me to hang up the phone and go look at my son who was asleep in his crib. That's all he said. I did this, and when I looked at this new, helpless, little life that was my son, I was suddenly overwhelmed with love and purpose and my troubles drifted away for that moment. That moment was all I needed to continue.

Rosita Perez
President: Creative Living Programs, Inc.
Mentor: Nancy Coey

No matter how skilled I am at what I do, I sometimes experience the fear, "Am I skilled enough?" In expressing that to Nancy, she said the following: "In the movie Hoosiers, the coach says to the basketball team, 'The distance to the basket is the same, even in the big arena.'"

I remembered that when I walked out in front of my largest audience to date: 7,700 folks. It calmed my soul. "The distance to the basket is the same!"

Les Brown
Motivational Speaker/Author
Mentor: Leroy Washington

Leroy always says—"Be the message that you give."

So now I make a conscious, deliberate, determined effort to walk my talk by setting high standards for myself and never stopping stretching and learning all I can to be a positive example for those whose lives I've touched through my work. These are words of encouragement that I provide not just lip service to, but make a part of my character.

Nido R. Qubein, Professional Speaker and Author
Chairman, Creative Services, Inc.
Mentor: My mother

She always instilled the belief in me that, to be a great person, I must first walk hand-in-hand and side-by-side with people who are great. When I came to America at age 17 with no connections, no money, and no knowledge of the English language, I sought out men and women who were great in their own fields and learned from them about life and living.

Ed Foreman
Business Entrepreneur
Mentor: Dr. Norman Vincent Peale

Peale says, as you speak, and as you think, express only hopeful, enthusiastic ideas. Become a "possibility thinker" and a "can-do" achiever. It will become natural to you to expect the good, the positive, and the beautiful in life. You'll automatically find enthusiasm and happiness and relaxation in yourself, and you'll start living a worry-free, happy, successful life! According to Peale:

"I found that it is as easy to program yourself for success as it is for mediocrity . . . the tragedy is that most people never understand nor discipline themselves to practice this success formula until it becomes a *habit*—part of their daily living . . . an automatic part of their subconscious mind. By developing a wholesome, cheerful, positive attitude, accompanied by action . . . plus specific goals, I've found health, wealth, and happiness."

Sheila Murray Bethel
Author
Mentor: Og Mandino

"Sheila, write about your passion! Write what you care most about! Write for yourself, don't worry if it sells, with passion and conviction it will sell!"

I did exactly what Og said. I wrote about where I see the strengths and weaknesses in leaders. I researched, studied, and interviewed leaders worldwide. I thought about what I want my sons to know and be as leaders. Og was right. My book, *Making a Difference: Twelve Qualities that Make You a Leader,* is now in its tenth printing.

Tony Alessandra
Speaker/Author
Mentor: Bill Gove

In 1982, Bill Gove told me to change my then-current "professorial" speaking style to mirror my natural personality—an entertaining and playful "in-your-face" New York Italian with a mischievous style.

I changed my speaking style according to Bill's advice and achieved overnight success. My bookings went up, repeat business increased, speaking fees shot up, and I was awarded the CPAE designation three years later from the National Speakers Association.

Danielle Kennedy
Author/Lecturer
Mentor: Tom Hopkins

Tom always said you shouldn't limit your market. Once you've dominated a niche, use the skills mastered and carry them across horizontally to other niches

I began speaking to and writing for real estate people. When I reached the top in speaker status, I focused on a new industry that needed my message. For example, direct sales (skin care, toys, pots and pans). Selling skills were needed across the board.

Joanne Slavik
Executive Administrative Assistant
Mentor: Thomas F. Crum

In times of conflict Thomas would always remind me to ask myself, do you want to be right, or do you want to be happy?

This principle has literally changed my understanding of what is "really" important—regarding all my relationships.

Gino Wickman
President, Floyd Wickman Courses
Mentor: My dad

When it comes to decisions, it's less important what you decide than it is that you decide.

John Hughes
Vice President, Client Relations
Mentor: Joe Girard

The elevator to success and wealth is out of order, you have to use the stairs. A step at a time.

BIBLIOGRAPHY

Adams, Joshua B. "My Mentor, Myself; Several Successful People Discuss Their Mentors," *Town & Country Monthly*, August 1994 (Vol. 148, No. 5171), p. 60.

Brown, Les. Personal interview with the authors, Fall 1995.

Brown, Robert L. "Million-Dollar Mentors Revisited," *Managers Magazine*, July 1991, p. 6.

Brown, Robert L. "Start with Structure; Creating a Mentoring Program," *Managers Magazine*, January 1993 (Vol. 68, No. 1), p. 16.

Dalessio, Anthony T. "Does It Work? What LIMRA Research Says about Mentoring," *Managers Magazine*, January 1993 (Vol. 68, No. 1), p. 10.

Fox, Roger N. "Staying Ahead: Mentors Can Pave the Way; Mentoring for Higher Agent Productivity," *Managers Magazine*, January 1994 (Vol. 69, No. 1—Back To Basics Column) p. 8.

Franey, Lynn. "Orange County Focus: Countywide, State Gives $398,000 for Mentor Program," *Los Angeles Times*, Orange County Edition, January 31, 1994 (Metro; Part B) p. 3.

French, Bob. "Young Entrepeneurs in Davie Get Business Owners As Mentors" *Fort Lauderdale Sun Sentinal*, Aug. 19, 1994 (Broward Edition) p. 4.

Gallese, Liz Roman. "Do Women Make Poor Mentors?" *Across The Board*, July 1993 (Vol. 30, No. 6) p. 23.

Geiger, Adrianne H. "Measures for Mentors" *Training and Development*, February 1992 (Vol. 46, No. 2) p. 65.

Gittler, Harvey. "Give Yourself a Present; Becoming a Mentor to an Employee." *Industry Week*, Dec. 6, 1993 (Vol. 242, No. 23) p. 18.

Grout, Pam. *The Mentoring Advantage*. Skillpath Publications, 1995.

Heery, William. "Corporate Mentoring Can Break the Glass Ceiling." *HR Focus* May 1994 (Vol. 71, No. 5) p. 17.

Herscher, Elaine. "Rewriting Rotten Life Scripts; Mentors Give Youths a Shot at Success." *San Francisco Chronicle*, Sept. 20, 1994 (Final Edition) p. A15.

Hinch, Gerald K. "Mentoring: Everyone Needs a Helping Hand." *The Public Manager: The New Bureaucrat*, March 22, 1993 (Vol. 22, No. 1) p. 31.

Hopkins, Tom. Personal interview with the authors, Fall 1995.

Kitchen, Patricia. "Don't Count on Mentor to Save Day; Mentor Relationships in Banking" *American Banker*, March 12, 1992 (Vol. 157, No. 49) p. 1.

Laabs, Jennifer J. "Mentors Offer Students the Tools for Job Success." *Personnel Journal*, March 1993 (Vol. 72, No. 3) p. 57.

Morris, Michele. "Is It Time to Leave Your Mentor?" *Executive Female*, March 1992 (Vol. 15, No. 2), p. 40.

Oates, Wayne E. "A Long Friendship; Spiritual Mentors." *The Christian Century*, January 19, 1994 (Vol. 111, No. 2) p. 38.

Public/Private Ventures. "First National Study of Mentoring Finds Nonprofit's Practices Superior." PR Newswire, April 27, 1993 (State and Regional News).

Ragins, Belle Rose, and John L. Cotton. "Gender and Willingness to Mentor in Organizations." *Journal of Management*, March 22, 1993 (Vol. 19, No. 1) p. 97.

Richards, Cindy. "Finding a Mentor Can Be the Key to Getting Ahead." *Chicago Sun-Times*, February 7, 1992 (Financial section; Working Women) p. 41.

Rogers, Beth. "Mentoring Takes a New Twist; the Training Investment" *HR Magazine;* Society for Human Resource Management, August 1992 (Vol. 37, No. 8) p. 48.

Sharp, Deborah. "Troubled Teen's Path Takes Another Twist/Florida Case Highlights Roadblocks Facing Mentors." *USA Today*, May 25, 1994 (Final, news section) p. 12A.

Soulsman, Gary. "Reflection Is the Key to Mentoring." *Wilmington News Journal*, June 30, 1992 (Gannett News Service).

Soulsman, Gary. "Prescribing the Right Mentor." *Wilmington News Journal*, June 30, 1992 (Gannett News Service).

Trebbe, Ann. "Cheryl Tiegs, a Model Mentor." *USA Today*, June 16, 1993 (Final, Life section), p. 2D.

Turban, Daniel B., and Thomas W. Dougherty. "Role of Protégé Personality in Receipt of Mentoring and Career Success." *Academy of Management Journal*, June 1994 (Vol. 37, No. 3) p. 688.

Tyler, J. Larry. "The Death of Mentoring; Executive Cooperation in the Health Care Industry." *Hospitals & Health Networks*, October 5, 1994 (Vol. 68, No. 19) p. 84.

Vander Weele, Maribeth. "Mentors Getting Their Act Together." *Chicago Sun-Times*, August 2, 1994 (Late Sports, Final Edition News) p. f.5.

Walthers, Catherine. "Reinventing the Circle: Mentoring Groups Are Taking Shape in Boston." *Boston Business Journal*, January 25, 1993 (Vol. 12, No. 49) p. S4.

Whitely, William T. Coetsier. "The Relationship of Career Mentoring to Early Career Outcomes." *Organization Studies*, June 22, 1993 (Vol. 14, No.3) p. 419.

Woolfolk, Betsy Cash. "The Business Market Is More Accessible than You May Think" *Life Insurance Selling*, December 1992, p. 58.

Zaslow, Jeffrey. "Mentors Succeed When Protégés Take on Role." *Chicago Sun-Times*, August 27, 1992 (Five Star Sports Final, Section 2; Features; All That Jazz) p. 49.

Ziglar, Zig. Personal interview with the authors, Fall 1995.

CONTRIBUTORS

The following individuals have been generous enough to contribute personal stories about mentoring that illustrate many of the points covered in this book. Each of them possesses a lifetime of unique experiences. All have given their personal time and emotional energy over the years to helping others grow personally or in their chosen career field. Thank you for sharing!

Jerry D. Anderson, CCIM

Jerry is a national real estate consultant who has marketed over $600 million of investment property in his 25 year career. He is coauthor of the bestselling audiotape program *Commercial Real Estate: How to Buy, Sell and Lease* by Nightingale Conant, and his book *Success Strategies for Investment Real Estate* is now a classic on the shelves of commercial real estate practitioners. He has presented to audiences in Australia, New Zealand, Canada, and all 50 states in the United States, and he is a frequent radio and television guest.

Debbie Bermont

Debbie Bermont, president of Source Communications, is a nationally recognized motivational and marketing speaker, consultant, and author. She has developed successful marketing programs for small businesses as well as for Fortune 500 companies. Debbie travels nationwide, speaking professionally on marketing and personal development topics. Source Communications is located at 2315 Kratky Rd., Suite. A, St. Louis, MO 63114, (314) 428-7999.

Dick Biggs

Dick Biggs is a dynamic keynote speaker, seminar leader, author of the popular book *If Life Is a Balancing Act, Why Am I So Darn Clumsy?* and producer of the six-cassette audio album *How To Balance Your*

Life. Contact him at Biggs Optimal Living Dynamics, 1001 Alpharetta St., Suite 100, Roswell, GA 30075, (770) 998-5452, FAX (770) 998-5513.

Ronald Bourque

Ron Bourque is a speaker, trainer, and consultant who specializes in helping organizations become more competitive using total quality management, just-in-time, process reengineering, and other techniques to improve performance. Bourque Associates International, 19 Cole Road, Windham, NH 03087 (603) 898-1871

Les Brown

Les Brown, CPAE, is considered "The Motivator." Les has a national reputation for getting audiences inspired, enlightened, and on their feet. He touches people. Les Brown Unlimited, P.O. Box 1646 (313) 961-1962.

Robert Brown

Mentoring Systems, Inc., 4001 MacArthur Blvd., Suite 300, Newport Beach, CA 92660.

Sam Cupp

Sam Cupp is an entrepreneur and the founder of Winning Futures, a mentoring program for high school students wishing to learn entrepreneurial skills. Sam can be contactd at (810) 205-2201.

Jeff Davidson

Jeff Davidson, MBA, CMC, is a popular speaker and the award-winning author of 22 books, including *Breathing Space: Living and Working at a Comfortable Pace in a Sped-Up Society*. For a complete resource list and for Jeff's keynote and breakout presentations, visit (http://www.BreSpace.com). You may also reach him at the Breathing Space® Institute, 2417 Honeysuckle Road, Suite 2A, Chapel Hill, NC 27514-6819, (919) 932-1996, fax (919) 932-9982.

Burt Dubin

Burt Dubin is the developer of the Speaking Success System, a powerful instrument for helping aspiring and professional speakers position, package, promote, and present themselves. He shows his clients how to create an endless parade of profitable speaking engagements—and he guarantees success. He may be reached at the Personal Achievement Institute in Arizona, 800-321-1225.

Christopher S. Frings

Christopher Frings, Ph.D., CSP, mixes magic and humor with cutting-edge information to provide exciting programs for audiences interested in mastering change and rethinking success, goal attainment, and time and stress management. He can be reached at Chris Frings & Associates, 633 Winwood Drive, Birmingham, AL 35226, (205) 823-5044, fax (205) 823-4283.

Devon Hansen

Devon Hansen, president of Inner Dynamics Consulting, is a nationally known speaker whose profound message has touched the hearts of thousands, empowering them to change. She is a talented and gifted professional who is the author of *Angry? Do You Mind If I Scream?* Inner Dynamics Consulting is located at 135 West Dorothy Lane, Suite 116, Kettering, OH 45429.

Tom Hopkins

Tom Hopkins is a master sales trainer. He has trained over two million students on five continents. His seminars, books, and tape programs receive rave reviews. Book sales alone are reaching the two million mark for one simple reason—the material works. For more information about Tom Hopkins, call toll free (800) 528-0446.

Rhoda Israelov

Rhoda Israelov, CFP, CLU, MS, is a financial advisor and a vice president of the Smith Barney brokerage firm. As a weekly columnist for the *Indianapolis Business Journal*, she offers financial advice to readers and is one of the most sought-after financial speakers in the midwest. Rhoda's primary work consists of managing the investments and insurance for over 400 business and individual clients. She is located at 1313 King's Cove Court, Indianapolis, Indiana 46260, (317) 844-6167, fax (317) 237-6417.

Millie Jarrett

Millie Jarrett owns the Nashville-based Speaking of Sales and Service company. She is a record-breaking salesperson, successful sales manager, and international sales trainer. Her high energy and love of the business reveals in people their magical ability to turn mediocre production into high-yield performance. She may be reached at 2307 Donna Hill Court, Nashville, TN 37214, (615) 889-5880, fax (615) 889-4266.

Michael Jeffreys

Michael Jeffreys is a motivational speaker and the author of four books including his latest, *Success Secrets of the Motivational Superstars.* In it he interviews 15 of the biggest names in the speaking world including Anthony Robbins, Wayne Dyer, Barbara De Angelis, Brian Tracy, Les Brown, Tom Hopkins, Mark Victor Hansen, and Jack Canfield. Michael can be reached at Powerful Magic Publishing, 1516 Purdue Ave. #7, Los Angeles, CA 90025, (310) 473-6291.

Herb Lloyd

Herb Lloyd owns Service Sales Consultants Seminars, Inc., a teaching, training, and consulting firm specializing in customer service and "counsel selling." He describes himself as a professional problem solver, and has given seminars and on-site training in sales and customer service for the Nestle, Nucorp, Amoco, and Chevron corporations as well as for other major businesses across the country. The address and phone numbers for Service Sales Consultants Seminars, Inc. is P.O. Box 943, Orem, UT 84059-0943, daytime, (801) 224-9404, evening (801) 754-3600, and toll-free (800) 209-6214; the fax is (801) 224-9273.

Richard McCloskey

Mentoring Systems, Inc., 4001 MacArthur Blvd., Suite 300, Newport Beach, CA 92660.

Larne Neuland

Larne's life is her testimony; she is author of *How To Win When Life Is Unfair* and *Have Message Will Travel*. P.O. Box 1937 Somerset West, 7129 Republic of South Africa.

M. Alice O'Connor

M. Alice O'Connor is a successful businesswoman who operates her own lobbying firm and professional speaking business in the Midwest. Alice considers herself to be self-taught and says mentors weren't around when she was breaking through "glass ceilings." She believes mentoring is a way of "giving back" all that a person has received in life, and she mentors young people and others who feel "powerless" in society. She belongs to the National Speakers Association. M. Alice O'Connor is located in the Verex Building, 150 E. Gilman, Suite 3100, Madison, WI 53703, (608) 255-7211, fax (608) 255-2203.

Sue Pivetta

Sue Pivetta is the owner of a training company for the 911 industry. She has published four books and a number of audio and video training tapes. As a motivational speaker, Sue encourages professional self-esteem, empowerment, and spirituality in life work. She can be reached at 2909 N. Starr, Tacoma, WA 98403, (800) 830-8228.

Mary Rudisill

Mary Rudisill is a member of the National Speakers Association. She is a professional speaker, trainer, and consultant on business relationship planning, customized customer service, and partnering team building. She also has authored a book on relationship skills, *Preventing a Broken Heart: Intimacy and Boundaries for Singles.* Mary may be reached at Mary Rudisill & Associates, P.O. Box 20441, Keizer, OR 97307, (503) 463-8446, fax (503) 463-5634, or e-mail MarywJC@aol.com.

Gary Silverman

Dr. Silverman is president of Motivational Medicine, Inc.™ He writes and produces medical audio tapes that are entertaining and enlightening. A member of the National Speakers Association, he frequently hosts medical talk radio and is a national spokesperson for many Fortune 500 pharmaceutical companies. He maintains a private practice in rheumatology in Scottsdale, Arizona. He can be reached at 3126 N. Civic Center Plaza, Scottsdale, AZ 85251, (602) 941-3991, fax (602) 949-9871.

Judy Tatelbaum

Judy Tatelbaum, MSW, an inspiring speaker and trainer, is an internationally recognized expert on grief and the author of the books *The Courage to Grieve* and *You Don't Have to Suffer.* She encourages people to overcome obstacles and to achieve fulfillment in their lives. She can be reached at P.O. Box 601, Carmel Valley, CA 93924, (408) 659-2270, fax (408) 659-2279.

Ken Wallace

Ken Wallace is a full-time professional speaker, trainer, consultant, and Methodist minister. He holds the Certified Seminar Leader (CSL) professional designation of the American Seminar Leaders Association, and his speaking, training, and consulting topics include ethics, communication, customer service, and leadership. He can be reached at One Hillcrest Drive, Carbondale, IL 62901, (800) 235-5690, fax (618) 457-4766.

Dottie Walters

Dottie Walters is a world-renowned expert on professional speaking and sales training, and she is the president and founder of the Walters International Speakers Bureau. She publishes *Sharing Ideas,* a leading publication of the international paid speakers bureau industry. She has authored numerous books including *Never Underestimate the Selling Power of a Woman, Speak and Grow Rich* with Lilly Walters, and *101 Simple Things to Grow Your Business and Yourself.* She has been interviewed on hundreds of radio and television shows and by the CNN and ABC networks. Dottie sold her 285-employee advertising business she built from scratch to concentrate on her speaking-related activities. Walters Speakers Services may be contacted at PO. Box 1120, Glendora, CA 91740, (818) 335-8069, fax (818) 335-6127, and e-mail call4spkr@aol.com.

Barb Wingfield

Barb Wingfield has been speaking professionally since 1987 and provides keynotes and seminars on communication and positive attitude. She is author of the book *Reasons to Say WOW!!!,* and she writes a monthly column for the *Ohio Country Journal.* She can be reached at Wingfield Enterprises, 10113 Road 110, Rushsylvania, OH 43347, (937) 468-2041, fax (937) 468-2273.

Betsy Cash Woolfolk

Betsy Cash Woolfolk is a senior partner of Virginia Asset Management and specializes in investments, IRAs, mutual funds, annuities, insurance, and deferred compensation plans. She holds a BS in management and marketing and is a qualifying and life member of Million Dollar Round Table and Court of the Table. In addition, she is a Chartered Life Underwriter (CLU) and a Chartered Financial Consultant (ChFC). Her mission statement is: "In servicing my clients, I shall, in the light of all circumstances, recommend that course of action which, had I been in the same situation, I would have applied to myself." She may be reached at Virginia Asset Management, 9211 Forest Hill Ave., Suite 202, Richmond, VA 23235, (804) 330-0711, fax (804) 330-0880.

Zig Ziglar

Zig Ziglar, CPAE, NSA is past director, writer, motivational teacher, and gives leadership seminars. The Zig Ziglar Corporation, 3330 Earhart, Suite 204, Carrollton, Texas 75006 (214) 233-9191.

FOR FURTHER INFORMATION

For more information on how Floyd Wickman or Terri Sjodin may be of service to you, your company, or your professional organization, or, to order additional copies of *Mentoring*, please write to:

Floyd Wickman & Associates
1707 West Big Beaver Road
Troy, MI, 48084
1 (800) 548-7733

or

Terri Sjodin
Sjodin Communications
P.O. Box 8998
Fountain Valley, CA 92728-8998
1-(714) 540-5594

INDEX

Other books of interest to you . . .

Making 2 + 2 = 5
22 Action Steps Leaders Take to Boost Productivity
John H. Zenger

"A real gem. I'm sometimes asked for one source on how to implement the management ideas I've written about. I now have the answer: Jack Zenger's book."

Bob Waterman, Coauthor of *In Search of Excellence*

Provides 22 actions any manager can use to turbocharge staff performance. Producing more with less is quickly becoming every company's motto, and Jack Zenger makes It possible by clearing away obstacles that have long obstructed worker productivity.
ISBN: 0-7863-1094-4

This Indecision is Final
32 Management Secrets of Albert Einstein, Billie Holiday, and a Bunch of Other People Who Never Worked 9 to 5
Barry Gibbons

If you are in any way connected to the perplexing world of big business—if you are an "also-ran," a "wannabe," a "has been" or even a "never was"—then *This Indecision is Final* is the book for you. Author Barry Gibbons' 25-year background in big business was the inspiration for this unique book. Armed only with his offbeat humor and insight, the candid former chairman and CEO of Burger King takes on almost everything related to the corporate world in a series of essays. Filled with inspiring ideas, caustic revelations, and profound irreverence, *This Indecision is Final* will make you laugh and ponder—and change your mind about you and your business.
ISBN: 0-7863-0838-9

Not Just for CEOs
Sure-Fire Success for the Leader In Each of Us
John H. Zenger

In an easy-to-read, straightforward style, author Jack Zenger offers an unparalleled guide to succeeding in business today. Uncovering the key behaviors of top performers, he describes precisely what makes them effective and outlines how you can follow in their path and shine. Zenger explains how everyone can provide leadership in their own area of work.
ISBN: 0-7863-0528-2